INCULTURATION

Working Papers on Living Faith and Cultures

edited by

ARIJ A. ROEST CROLLIUS, S.J.

VII

This issue has been published in collaboration with the Centre for Coordination of Research of the International Federation of Catholic Universities (F.I.U.C) and with the help of the Konrad Adenauer Foundation.

CENTRE "CULTURES AND RELIGIONS" - PONTIFICAL GREGORIAN UNIVERSITY

R. Hardawiryana, A.M. Varaprasadam, K. Bertens,
J. Banawiratma, M.E. Chiong-Javier, P. Knecht,
J. Dinh Duc Dao

BUILDING THE CHURCH
IN PLURICULTURAL ASIA

ROME 1986

Robert Hardawiryana had his theological training in Holland and Rome and has been teaching theology in Yogyakarta since 1961, at what is at present the Theological Faculty "Vedabhakti". He also teaches at the Higher Catechetical Institute "Pradnyawidya". He is consultor of the Indonesian Bishops' Conference and of the FABC. In Universities in various continents he has been guest-lecturer.

☆

Arul M. Varaprasadam, is an Indian Jesuit, former provincial of Madurai Province. He has a Master's from the Loyola University of Chicago. Was a member of the Inculturation Commission which worked out an outline for Jesuit training attuned to the Indian context. Since 1980 he is editor of a Tamil monthly dealing with issues of social justice.

☆

Kees Bertens is Director of Atma Jaya Center for Philosophy and Ethics at Atma Jaya Catholic University, Jakarta, Indonesia. He wrote and translated into Indonesian several books on systematic philosophy and the history of philosophy.

☆

Joannes B. Banawiratma, born in Java in 1946, made his studies in Indonesia and at Innsbruck University. He teaches theology at Vedabhakty Faculty in Yogyakarta, and is member of the Commission for Ecumenism and Dialogue of the Indonesian Bishops' Conference. He is the author of several studies on actual theological problems.

☆

Maria Elena Chong-Javier teaches at De La Salle University in Manila. She has done extensive anthropological research in various parts of the Philippines and is the author of several studies on anthropology.

☆

V

Peter Knecht, born in Switzerland, 1937. Member of Divine Word Missionaries (SVD). Studied Philosophy in St. Gabriel, Mödling (Austria), and Theology at the Gregoriana, Rome. In Japan since 1966. Did doctoral studies in cultural anthropology at the University of Tokyo. Teaches Anthropology of Religion at Nanzan University, Nagoya, since 1978. Fieldwork experience in rural Japan, focussed on beliefs and religious attitudes of the household and village level. Editor of Asian Folklore Studies.

☆

Joseph Dinh Duc Dao is a Vietnamese priest. He is now Vice-Director of the International Center of Missionary Animation and teaches in the Missiology Faculty of the Pontifical Urban University (Rome); he is a regular contributor to various periodicals. His most recent book was published by EMI: "La Sposa sul Monte. Il contributo dell'Asia per una Chiesa contemplativa e missionaria."

TABLE OF CONTENTS

PRESENTATION

INCULTURATION: THE CHRISTIAN EXPERIENCE AMIDST CHANGING CULTURES

From September 22 till 26, the Center for Coordination of Research of the F.I.U.C. had brought together 25 specialists of various disciplines, for a common study on the phenomenon of inculturation. The symposium consisted in four days of intense work.

In a first stage, the process of inculturation was studied from various points of view: biblical, theological, catechetical, historical, anthropological, etc. At the end of this stage, a convergence of opinions and insights manifested itself as to the perennial character of the encounter between Church and cultures, throughout the history of Christianity and also the newness of this encounter in our days, in its plurality of contexts and the urgency of reconciling pluralism with unity in the Church.

During a second stage, an effort was made to identify those areas and situations which required more apostolic and pastoral discernment and more theological and academic research. Since all continents and nearly as many disciplines as participants were represented, this search resulted in a lively and fruitful discussion. The areas identified as "priority areas" were those of socio-political justice, the role of women, ecclesiology, religious pluralism.

In a concluding session, concrete proposals were formulated in order to promote the concerted effort of the Catholic Universities all over the world in contributing to effective action in the "priority areas".

The unique setting of Tantur, half way between Jerusalem and Bethlehem, the efficiency of its direction and staff and the contacts with local scholars have contributed to making this Symposium a very special experience for all who took part in it.

The present volume of INCULTURATION publishes some of the papers of the Jerusalem symposium. We have brought together here those papers which have more directly to do with inculturation in Asia. To these have been added two other papers on inculturation in Asia which were read at a Jesuit seminar in Yogyakarta (Indonesia) in 1983, and which complete very well the five other papers.

The first contribution of this issue is by Robert Hardawiryana, who presents a little "summa" on inculturation in the pluricultural situation that is characteristic for Asia as a whole and for most Asian countries in particular.

This study is followed by a presentation of the growing of the Church in the ethnic, religious and cultural pluralism of India today. This paper has been read in Jerusalem by Arul M. Varaprasadam.

The following two studies deal more directly with inculturation in Indonesia. The one by Kees Bertens in a more general way and the one by J.B. Banawiratma has a more immediately theological approach.

An anthropological study on the cultural change provoked by the preaching of the Gospel has been presented by Maria Elena Chiong-Javier, who studies the case of the Hanunuo Mangyan in the Philippines.

Peter Knecht highlights the problem of ancestors' worship in the Japanese religious and cultural consciousness.

The series is concluded by an in-depth study on prayer and inculturation in the Asian context. Joseph Dinh Duc Dao presents the case of Zen meditation.

I would like to remind that these papers are published as working papers and not as the last word on the matter at hand. These publications intend to stimulate further research in view of a fruitful and concordant action in this endeavour of inculturation.

ARIJ A. ROEST CROLLIUS, S.J.

X

Robert Hardawiryana, S.J.

BUILDING THE CHURCH OF CHRIST IN A PLURICULTURAL SITUATION

Introduction

As early as in 1659 the Congregation for the Faith warned that nothing could be more foolish than to want to bring France, Spain, Italy or any other European country to China.

> "That is not what you have to transplant. What you have to transplant is the Faith that neither despises nor destroys the customs and usages of any country" [1]

The Constitutions of our Society insist that attention be paid to the circumstances of country, place, language, different mentalities, and personal temperaments. These passages as well as many instructions testify to Ignatius' constant concern for the concrete situation.[2] Faithful to the tradition of our Society upheld by missionaries in the past — Xavier, Ricci, de Nobili and many others — this seminar aims at deepening our theological insight in what in the 1950's was called "incorporative accommodation",[3] now largely known as "inculturation", the problem of how to hold on to the concrete and the particular, even to the last detail, "without renouncing the breadth and universality of those human values", —

---

[1] Quoted by Karl MÜLLER SVD, *Coresponsibility in Evangelisation*, in: *Toward a New Age in Mission, The Good News of God's Kingdom to the Peoples of Asia*, ed. by the Theological Conference Office, International Mission Congress, National Printing Company, Manila 1981, vol. II book III (abbrev. *IMC II*) p. 241. Reference is made to H. JEDIN, *Weltmission und Kolonialismus*, Saeculum 9 (1958) pp. 393-404.

[2] For references see: *On Inculturation. A Letter of Father General Pedro Arrupe to the whole Society*, Rome 14 May 1978, Cur. Gen. 78/5, p. 4.

[3] Cf. K. MÜLLER SVD, art. cit., footnote 5 p. 252, with reference to J. MÜLLER, *Missionarische Anpassung als theologisches Prinzip*, Münster 1973. For theological reasons the terms "adaptation" and "accommodation" are ever more abandoned as less appropriate.

we may add: of the Gospel values, — which not even the totality of all cultures can express and live exhaustively.[4] Hopefully our concerted theological reflection will prove helpful in finding the pastoral approach proper to each of our countries in building the Church of Christ.

Vatican II particularly invited "the young churches" to show initiative and creativity and to discover solutions for their own problems.[5] Yet they often seem to be neither adequately responsive, courageous nor mature; many still look to Rome to spell out in detail all that has to be done at home. National and regional hierarchies have started to function for common pastoral programmes and for better coordination within the universal Church. Yet they still do not enjoy sufficient freedom and initiative to decide nationally or regionally their own problems. Not seldom it happens that local issues are placed before regional bodies and regional issues before universal bodies, and detailed guidance is expected from such bodies. Hence it is all the more necessary to carry out Paul VI's invitation: to make every effort and give serious attention to the evangelization of cultures.[6]

Too many are the problems and the challenges we are to cope with: how is inculturation to be understood theologically? how to deal with religions and religious values, deeply interwoven in our cultures and decisive in the lives of our peoples? what has inculturation to do with modernization and the problem of poverty and injustice, particularly in developing countries? what are the challenges to be met along the process of inculturation? what is the role of the christian community in that process?

---

[4] See: P. ARRUPE SJ, *On Inculturation*, p. 4.

[5] See e.g. "*Ad Gentes*" (AG) 15: "From the very start, the Christian community should be so formed that it can provide for its own necessities insofar as this is possible". AG.6 stresses "the variety of situations", "the circumstances", on which "the appropriate actions and tools must be brought to bear". Concerning Liturgy see "*Sacrosanctum Concilium*" (SC) 37-40.

[6] Cf. "*Evangelii Nuntiandi*" (EN) 20.

Chapter one: INCULTURATION: THE PASCHAL MYSTERY REALIZED IN HUMAN SOCIETY

Vatican II describes culture in the sociological and ethnological sense as comprising "all those factors by which man refines and unfolds his manifold spiritual and bodily qualities", etcetera.[7] It also delineates the dialectical relationship between man as called to salvation and his cultural situation:

"Just as human activity proceeds from man, so it is ordered toward man. For when a man works he not only alters things and society, he develops himself as well. He learns much, he cultivates his resources, he goes outside of himself and beyond himself".[8]

Culture is a world-view, a complex of symbolic expressions, a way of life. Actually it is a complex of subcultures. The elite, the middle class, the poor, the workers, the urban proletariat, the youth, all have their subcultures, each with its specific characteristics and tensions.[9] Hence the necessity of profound and thoroughgoing interdisciplinary studies, lest any approach to a culture might be superficial, subjective, fanciful, unbalanced, and consequently experiments of inculturation become haphazard, makeshift, even counterproductive.

On the other hand one might have to be on the *qui vive* as regards "systematic" pictures of "classical" cultures (worldviews, values, attitudes, other cultural expressions), since they might correspond to none of the contemporary subcultural expressions. For purposes of inculturation they might not be that relevant.[10] We get acquainted with a culture by being inserted into it, by "empathy" in living contact with the people, because the most intimate values can be perceived only from within.

---

[7] Cf. "*Gaudium et Spes*" (GS) 53. Particularly relevant for our theme: GS.57 on "faith and culture"; GS.58 on "the many links between the Gospel and culture".

[8] Cf. GS.35; also GS.25 on the interdependence of the human person and society.

[9] Cf. M. AMALADOSS SJ, *Inculturation and Tasks of Mission*, in *IMC.II*, p. 34f.

[10] M. AMALADOSS SJ considers this as "a common failing in the past in Asia", ibidem.

How about Christianity as brought to us by our missionaries? Is it a "culture"? The Gospel, and hence evangelization, are not identical with culture or with any cultures. But the fact that Christian faith is capable of permeating them all[11] makes it not always easy, at least at the level of concrete formulation and of practice, to distinguish between the specifically Christian elements and the cultural contribution, as already the first Christian elements and the cultural contribution, as already the first Christian communities experienced.[12]

This makes us the more aware of the complexity of inculturation problems, which by their very nature cannot be resolved simply by general rules but in the light of concrete and particular experiences.[13]

Inculturation is not to be treated merely in anthropological or sociological terms, but as a genuinely theological issue. Since it brings the Gospel into the heart of people in their concrete life-situation, in order to transform standards of judgment, reigning values, interests, patterns of thinking, motives and ideals,[14] it belongs to the very core of evangelization.[15] It is to be achieved after the model of the mystery of *trinitarian life,* where Father and Son have everything in common because they exist in mutual giving and receiving and live in the perfection of sharing which is the Spirit.

Evangelization, essentially Christ's mission continued in time through the Church, is concerned with *the kingdom of God*[16] of

---

[11] Cf. EN.20; of course without becoming subject to any culture.

[12] Cf. *A Working Paper on Inculturation,* in: *On Inculturation,* p. 16.

[13] Cf. *The First Bishops' Institute for Missionary Apostolate of the Federation of Asian Bishops' Conferences* (BIMA I), 19-27 July 1978, Baguio City, Philippines, in: *IMC.II,* p. 22.

[14] Cf. EN.20.

[15] Cf. BIMA I, in: *IMC.II,* p. 22.

[16] Cf. our article: *The Missionary Dimensions of the Local Church. Asia and Indonesia,* in: *Mission in Dialogue* (The SEDOS Research Seminar on the Future of Mission, March 8-19, 1981, Rome, Italy), ed. by M. MOTTE F.M.M. and J.R. LANG M.M., Orbis Books, Maryknoll, New York 1982 (abbrev. *MD*), p. 34; A. PANTIN C.S.Sp.-M. de VERTEUILT C.S.Sp., *Mission in the Local Church in Relation to other Religious Traditions. Trinidad,* in: *MD* p. 368; Chr. SIDOTI, *The Liberation and Jusitice Dimension of the Mission of the Local Church. The Australian Church,* in: *MD.* p. 602 f.

which the Gospel indicates certain concrete signs.[17] There are two approaches in inculturation depending on how the relationship between the Church and the kingdom is conceived:

When the Church is considered coextensive with God's kingdom, the world (hence also culture) has to fit into the Church (rather than the Church making its way within the world). Culture is attended to to the extent of its being useful for missionaries to preach the Good News. If however culture does not prove to be helpful, it must be put aside. Would not some sort of ecclesiocentrism still underly Vatican II's view on inculturation, where in the decree on the Missionary Activity of the Church it says:

> "Thus in imitation of the plan of the Incarnation, the young Church, rooted in Christ and built up on the foundation of the apostles, takes to herself in a wonderful exchange all the riches of the nations which were given to Christ as an inheritance".[18]

The Church may be the vanguard of God's kingdom. But the reality of the kingdom is a more encompassing and yet to be realized phenomenon. Evangelization is essential to the Church's growth into that fuller reality. But the Church grows toward the fulfillment of God's kingdom on earth, rather than the world and its cultures growing into the fuller reality of the Church. Missionaries, therefore, need to conform their understanding of the Gospel message to the reality of those to whom they are sent. In this approach inculturation "is not just a step that might be helpful in a deeper understanding of the Gospel" (according to the former approach), but is "imperative in order that the event of the Word might take place at all".[19]

---

[17] Cf. A. PIERIS SJ, *Mission in the Local Church in Relation to other Religious Traditions. The non-Semitic Religions of Asia*, in: *MD*. p. 436-438; Chr. SIDOTI, art. cit., ibidem.

[18] Cf. AG.22, with reference to Ps. 2,8. Also: AG.6: "The specific purpose of the missionary activity is evangelization and the planting of the Church among those peoples and groups where she has not yet taken root". We would rather say: the Church is *in itself* being built and concretely shaped by *rendering service* to society in all aspects of life; in other words: by reaching out beyond itself.

[19] Cf. R.J. SCHREITER C.P.P.S., *A Framework for a Discussion of Inculturation*, in *MD*, p. 545.

The Incarnation of the Son is the primary motivation and perfect pattern for inculturation. In virtue of the Word made flesh, the Church must become part of society "for the same motive which led Christ to bind Himself ... to the definite social and cultural conditions of those human beings, among whom he dwelt" (cf. AG. 10). By being incarnate as intimately as possible the christian community is enriched with many cultural values, at the same time offering them Christ's message and the resources for a new life. None of those values may be ignored or suppressed; all must be cultivated and assimilated. The Church fosters and takes to itself the ability, resources and customs of each people while purifying, strengthening and enobling them (cf. LG. 13). Thus christian life not only is expressed through elements proper to the culture in question (this would be merely superficial accommodation). It becomes "a principle that animates, directs and unifies the culture, transforming and remaking it so as to bring about 'a new creation'".[20] Christ's continued mission, constitutive for the Church,[21] must be an incarnated reality.[22] It is dynamic by virtue of his disciples' understanding of the Word of God as an event.[23]

---

[20] Cf. P. ARRUPE SJ, *On Inculturation*, pp. 1-2.

[21] Cf. J.H. SASAKI, *The Missionary Dimensions of the Local Church. Japan,* in *MD,* pp. 100, 103; J. REILLY SJ, *Christian Mission and Ecumenical Relations in the Context of the Local Church. Australia,* in *MD.* p. 203; R.C. ROSSIGNOL ,.e.p., *What is the Role of Missionary Institutes?* in *MD.* p. 305; J.N.M. WIJNGAARDS M.H.M.-P. DIRVEN M.H.M., *Wayfarers in a New Age,* in *MD.* p. 317; Boka di MPASI LONDI SJ, *Mission in the Local Church in Relation to other Religious Traditions.* Zaire, in *MD.* p. 356; A. PIERIS SJ, art. cit. 427.

[22] Cf. P.A. BIEN-AIMÉ O.P., *The Missionary Dimensions of the Local Church. Haiti,* in *MD.* p. 4; L. BOSETO, *Christian Mission and Ecumenical Relations in the Context of the Local Church. The Pacific,* in *MD.* p. 172, 174; J. MUTISO-MBINDA, *Christian Mission and Ecumenical Relations ...,* East-Africa, in *MD.* pp. 187 f; J.T. BOBERG S.V.D., *The Mission of the Local Church and the Missionary Institutes. The United States of America,* in *MD.* pp. 232-233; Ph. NKIERE KENA C.I.C.M., *The Birth of a "New People". The Mission of the Disciples of Jesus Christ in Today's Black Africa,* in *MD.* p. 291.

[23] Cf. J.H. SASAKI, art. cit., in *MD.* p. 103; H.H. HERRARA, *The Experience of the Local Church of Chimbote, Peru,* in *MD.* pp. 136 f; Ph. NKIERE KENA C.I.C.M., art. cit., in *MD.* pp. 290 f; Boka di MPASI LONDI SJ, art. cit., in *MD.* pp. 358-360; P. KWASI SARPONG, *The Mission of the Local Church and the Inculturation of the Gospel. Ghans,* in *MD.* p. 543; R.J. SCHREITER C.P.P.S., art. cit., in *MD.* pp. 545-547.

Inculturation transforms the life of the community from within. It gives rise to new patterns of relationships and behavior, a new way of worship, a new way of theologizing. Therefore, "only an inculturated lifepraxis experience can be the source of an inculturated spirituality, worship, theology and proclamation".[24]

The mystery of Incarnation reached its accomplishment in *the Paschal mystery*. Since our cultural situation is deeply affected by sin, our redemption in this mystery involves essentially our crucifixion, our conversion to new life in Christ. So also each culture to be taken up in Christ must share in his death and resurrection. It must be purified, strengthened, perfected and restored in Christ,[25] in order to be able to respond fully to the Holy Spirit and to be a genuine expression of christian life. The transformation effected through evangelization involves a certain rupture through a process of *"kenosis"*.[26] Missionaries have first to lay aside their own culture, their particular way of looking at things, and to allow themselves to take on their newly adopted culture; a real death with all its pains, perhaps a harder sacrifice than the toilsome labor of their predecessors in the past. While searching for the Gospel's relevance to actual life situations, the christian community is continuously challenged "to die to itself, to its limited vision, inadequate attitudes and imperfect cultural values, and constantly strive towards a closer fidelity to the Gospel".[27] Only thus it can assume its responsibility at the local level, "with freedom, energy, and creativity, with the risk also of making mistakes which will be corrected in the light of experience".[28] Even the Gospel has to die constantly to its limited historical expression,

---

[24] M. AMALADOSS SJ, art. cit., *IMC.II,* pp. 36 f.

[25] Cf. GS.58. Noteworthy is the reference made to Pius XI: "OIt is necessary never to lose sight of the fact that the objective of the Church is to evangelize, not to civilize. If it civilizes, it is for the sake of evangelization", *Semaines sociales de France,* Versailles 1936, pp. 461-462, in W.M. ABBOTT SJ - J. GALLAGHER, *The Documents of Vatican II,* America Press 1966, p. 264.

[26] Cf. Boka di MPASI LONDI SJ, art. cit., in *MD.* pp. 357-360; J.J. KNIGHT S.V.D., *Mission in the Local Church in Relation to other Religious Traditions. Melanesia,* in *MD.* pp. 392-411.

[27] Cf. M. AMALADOSS SJ art. cit., *IMC.II* p. 37.

[28] Cf. *A Working Paper on Inculturation,* in: *On Inculturation* p. 18.

in order to remain true to itself and to become meaningful to actual life through interpretation.[29]

The process of inculturation receives its lifegiving power from the mutual self-gift of Father and Son, *the Holy Spirit,* sent by the risen Christ. With his action the Spirit penetrates our pluricultural situation, and impels all men towards union with Christ. Hence in implementing our mission of evangelization we must be docile to the Spirit, sensitive to what he is working not only within the Church, but also within our entire society, in the hearts of all men. It is in the Spirit, that man in giving is like the Father (cf. Mt. 5,44) and in receiving like the Son (cf. Mt. 25,40), and that communion exists after the pattern of the Divine union (Jn. 17,22). The Spirit is present along the whole process of inculturation revealing the richness both of Christ's mystical Body and of the cultures in which the Word event is to take place. The Spirit gives validity to the plurality verified within the unity of the Church, and testifies to the wholeness of the Church realized in so many particularities, to its "catholicity" (cf. LG. 13).

It is in the Spirit that in time and space is continued and articulated the dialogue of salvation initiated by God and brought to a culmination, when he uttered his Word in a very concrete historical situation,[30] that dialogue between God and man and among men themselves is implied in every process of inculturation. This process

"starts with the personal vital encounter with the risen Lord, the transforming experience of reconciliation and salvation, and the consequent inner urge and will to share with others this transforming experience by the proclamation of the Word, gathering of a community of believers and celebration of the Eucharist. The worshipping community recognizing and experiencing the Lord in the celebration is filled with untold dynamism to share this Christic

---

[29] Since the Gospel comes as already embodied in a particular culture, the process of inculturation implies "discovering the Gospel in the form in which it comes embodied through the process of interpretation", and "re-expressing it in new cultural forms", cf. M. AMALADOSS SJ, art. cit. *IMC.II,* p. 34.

[30] Cf. *A Letter from the Participants* (of BIMA I) *to the Bishops of Asia,* n. 9, in *IMC.II* p. 29. E.D. Piryns C.I.C.M., *Contextual Theology: the Japanese Case,* Philippiniana Sacra vol. XIV, n. 40 (1979) pp. 141-144.

experience in their lifecontacts through humble service and total involvement. Thus the worshipping community becomes an evangelizing community, a community of witness and service in love. This process of dynamic and transforming experience goes on continuously till the universal community is realized".[31]

In the Spirit we discover the "seeds of the Word" ("*semina Verbi*") hidden in the cultures and the living traditions.[32] Of course, anthropological studies and interdisciplinary research are required in order to establish criteria for discerning those seeds which have fostered some Gospel values in various forms. Still, we need God's Spirit to guide us in this discernment, in making "implicit Christianity explicit", thereby deepening the understanding we have both of the Gospel message and of our own lives.

Continuing the mystery of Incarnation accomplished in a very particular context, the Church as a whole is marked by the richness of Pentecost, presenting the paradoxical characteristics of universality and particularity. This is what happens, when Jesus Christ, the Son of God, enters history as an individual while at the same time transcending all particularity. Because of his genuine incarnation as a man with a real family history all creation will be cought up, in plurality and in unity, in his paschal glory.

The mystery of the Church is one, total and universal. Its concrete realization when at mission is varied, multiple and particular. The particular Church, in which the Church of Christ is truly present and operative (cf. CD.11), is the embodiment of Christ's mystycal Body amidst the actual conditions of people. Each christian community, expressing itself in terms of its own culture and traditions, in its own "language", becomes an epiphany of the universal Church which it provides with definite and recognizable features. It should live in due autonomy and freedom and develop responsibility, originality, creativity and inventiveness. Thus based on social, cultural, religious plurality, ecclesial pluralism "is a

---

[31] Cf. D.S. AMALORPAVADASS, *A Theology of Basic Christian Communities and Ministries, IMC.II,* pp. 204 f.

[32] The expression "seeds of the Word" occurs in AG.11; in the Taipei Statement of FABC 1974, n. 27; and in John Paul II's encyclical letter "*Redemptor Hominis*", 11.

guarantee of the unity and universality of the Church as well as of its authenticity and credibility".[33] In expressing this universality in particularity the communion of faith is an important factor.[34]

Chapter two: INCULTURATION: RESPONDING TO ALL MEN'S QUEST OF THE SAVING GOD

Now that we have considered the paschal mystery in its trinitarian structure as the theological basis of building the christian community in a pluricultural situation, we proceed to our reflection on two dimensions of the inculturation of christian faith. While leaving the sociocultural dimension for the next chapter, here we focus our attention on how to deal with religious values within culture.

Communion in christian faith is fostered within the cultural situation. The culturally affected expressions of faith are a constitutive element in the "interiorization" of faith and reflect the richness of the divine Mystery. Needless to say how important it is to pay particular attention to the religious factor as "the animating principle of culture and the most important element of the worldview expressed in a culture".[35]

Since the second quarter of this century theological reflection has progressively concentrated upon people of other faiths and beliefs and instilled respect particularly for them in their religious identity. Catholic theology progressed from considering the "non-christian" as a "being of pure nature" deprived of any grace

---

[33] Cf. D.S. AMALORPAVADASS, art. cit., *IMC.II*, p. 205.

[34] Cf. P.A. BIEN-AIMÉ O.P., art. cit., in *MD.* p. 9; P. D'SOUZA, *The Missionary Dimensions of the Local Church. India*, in *MD.* p. 25; Tissa BALASURIYA O.M.I., *Secular Society and the Kingdom of God*, in *MD.* pp. 115 f; M.A. ODUYOYE, *The Mission of the Church and Nigerian Realities*, in *MD.* pp. 150 f; L. BOSETO, art. cit., in *MD.* p. 184; J.T. BOBERG S.V.D. art. cit., in *MD.* p. 240; C.T. HALLY S.S.C., *The Mission of the Local Church and the Missionary Institutes*, in *MD.* pp. 245-247, 259 f; A. PANTIN C.S.Sp.-M. de VERTEUIL C.S.Sp., art. cit., in *MD.* pp. 370 f; A. NAMBIAPARAMBIL C.M.I., *Mission in the Local Church in Relation to other Religious Traditions. India*, in *MD.* p. 423; J. GREMILLION, *The Regional Church of North America*, in *MD.* p. 469; Chr. Sidoti, art. cit., in *MD.* pp. 602 f.

[35] Cf. M. AMALADOSS SJ , art. cit., in *IMC.II*, p. 36.

("extra Ecclesiam nulla salus"!) to seeing him as created in Christ and called to salvation.

> "Since Christ died for all men, and since the ultimate vocation of man is in fact one and divine, we ought to believe that the Holy Spirit in a manner known only to God offers to every man the possibility of being associated with this paschal mystery".[36]

Thus people of other religions have been raised "theologically" to the level of brotherhood, to be accepted fully as fellow wayfarers towards God's kingdom.[37]

In Asia, whrere Christians are an insignificant minority in terms of numbers, the dialogue of life with the poor referred to by the Taipei assembly of FABC in 1974 is growing into a dialogue of life with people of other religions, "in order to make all people, both Christians and non-Christians, respond together to the poor irrespective of caste or creed".[38] And indeed, Asia, "where there is still a strong bond between religion and culture, is a privileged place, where the whole Church can draw inspiration for remedying the tragic situation of so many parts of the world where faith is divorced from the life-experience of the people".[39]

Religion has not only to do with the world-view dimension of culture. While religion certainly has as its component some sort of "a system of beliefs" more or less clearly spelled out, for our purpose of inculturation closer attention is called for to religion as an activity not to be distinctly differentiated from cultural patterns or transferred from one culture to another. In our context it is even far more important to take notice of religious practice than of religious belief.[40]

---

[36] Cf. GS.22, quite in harmony with Vatican II's Declaration "*Nostra Aetate*".

[37] Cf. P. ROSSANO, *Problème théologique du dialogue entre le christianisme et les religions non chrétiennes,* in: Bulletin: Secretariatus pro non Christianis, XIII (1978) 2, p. 88.

[38] Cf. *Reflections at the Conclusion of BISA VI on "the Challenge to human Development in the 1980's": Response of the Church in Asia ad 3.* (BISA VI was held in Kandy, Sri Lanka, 4-8 February 1983.

[39] Cf. BIMA I, in *IMC.II,* p. 22.

[40] Cf. R.J. SCHREITER C.P.P.S., art. cit., in *MD.* p. 551.

The people around us have been for centuries largely predetermined and are now conditioned by prevailing religious values expressed in a particular symbolism requiring the profound "religious sense" of the people themselves to be grasped as meaningful. These values may be very persistent at least as an undercurrent in confrontation with external, foreign or alien, religious influences, although at the same time there may be some vagueness or indistinctness about them. Often enough for outsiders it is not easy to perceive and appreciate "popular religiosity" and all that it comprises.

Traditional religious beliefs and practices are so such part of the cultural fiber of a people, that they are not automatically wiped off by baptism or transformed into Gospel values. When, therefore, the evangelization process has not been sufficiently transforming,[41] people have in moments of crisis recourse to those traditional forms of religion.

Since religion and religious activity are a vital element in the complex of cultural patterns, for the purpose of inculturation one may not separate religion from culture in the analytic process. Using the same mode of analysis in studying both will serve the inculturation process in many ways. Firstly, when religion and culture are taken as one reality, the introduction of Christianity need not alienate people from their own culture. The inculturation process steadily transforms at once both religion and culture from within. Accepting the Gospel one is convinced to live his culture better than before. Sudden ruptures with the cultural past are easier avoided. Secondly, since religious practices tend to have a more comprehensive and deeper meaning for life than formulations of a worldview or a beliefsystem, there is less danger of missing what actually is going on in a culture when one attends to practices.

Besides, since religion in many areas is almost inextricably woven into the cultural fabric,[42] using the same tools for cultural

---

[41] R.J. Schreiter C.P.P.S. proposes three guiding principles for the dynamics of transformation, viz., inclusion (based on Jesus' invitation to all to become part of the kingdom), judgment (cf. Jesus' call to repentance and conversion in order to enter the kingdom), and service (cf. Jesus' teaching as to how his disciples should relate to the reality of the kingdom), art. cit., in *MD. pp. 546 f.*

[42] E.g., to be Thai is to be Buddhist.

14

and religious analysis allows development of concepts of "double belonging".[43]

Moreover, using the same standards for cultural and religious analysis makes the problem of syncretism or fusion of religion and culture easier to deal with. Since such a fusion seems to be common, perhaps even necessary, the real issue is not whether such a syncretism will take place, but rather, who will control the process.

In short, as R.J. Schreiter C.P.P.S., puts it:

> "Using different methods of analysis for religion and culture reflects a bias about their relation coming out of particular North Atlantic circumstances. Both have to do with values both have to do with coping with life, both have verbal expressions that incorporate those values with the experience of life".[44]

Vatican II's declaration "*Nostra Aetate*" teaches us which attitude to take in relating with our brothers of other faiths and religious beliefs: fellowship and love (NA.1); sincere respect, readiness to engage in dialogue and collaboration and to promote the spiritual and moral goods among them (NA.2); esteem, readiness to understand (NA.3); understanding and respect (NA.4); to act in a brotherly way and to keep peace with them (NA.5).[45]

Whatever goodness and truth is found in those religions is considered as "a preparation for the gospel", "given by Him who enlightens all men so that they may finally have life" (LG.16). It is a matter of a multiform revelation transcending the simple "natural possibility of knowing God", while not yet attaining the order of the historical revelation found in the Old and New Testaments. But again it is the way people respond in faith to that revelation and express that faith in religious practices that matters first.

As the "prolongation" of the mystery of the Incarnation reaching its acme in the paschal mystery, inculturation is a problem everywhere and at all times. The north Atlantic secularistic situation also is a particular source of concern perhaps no less grave than the Third World. Yet the African and Asian situations respectively pose their particular problems.

---

[43] E.g., the concept of being a "Buddhist Christian".
[44] Cf. R.J. Schreiter C.P.P.S., art. cit., in *MD*. pp. 551 f.
[45] The same attitude is inculcated in LG.16.

15

To start with explicit religious tenets and subsequently to take up corresponding religious practice means that we might overlook major aspects of religious activity in the inculturation process. As in the case of non-institutional religious beliefs, some religious practices may not be correlated to very definite doctrines. There may be even practices seemingly contrary to stated beliefs.[46]

John Paul II's encyclical "*Redemptor Hominis*" (1979) invites us to come closer together with people of other faiths[47] and to have a positive outlook on their religions.[48] Every christian community needs continually to deepen its inculturation of the Gospel by confronting traditional religious values and practices with its faith in Jesus Christ and by transforming them. This cannot be carried out by outsiders, but must be implemented by the community itself. For the christian involved in dialogue it is imperative to be open to whatever is good and true coming from his fellow brother, even before giving him the testimony of all that God has done in Jesus Christ. Quite perfect is the definition given by the Indian Episcopal Commission for Dialogue:

> "Dialogue is the response of Christian faith in Gòd's saving presence in other religious traditions and the expression of firm hope of their fulfilment in Christ".[49]

Culture might challenge formulations of our christian faith, but interreligious dialogue can, for many, challenge the very core of that faith.

---

[46] E.g., in this country, where autochthonous beliefs until now have persisted as an undercurrent, and where Islam was introduced 6 or 7 centuries after the flourishing period of Hinduism and Buddhism, there are quite a few religious practices among so called "muslims", that are actually opposed to the doctrine of Islam. On recourse to traditional religious rituals on the part of christians, cf. also P.A. BIEN-AIMÉ O.P., art. cit. (Haiti) in *MD*. pp. 11f; M.A. ODUYOYE, art. cit. (Nigeria) in *MD*. p. 146; Boka di MPASI LONDI SJ, art. cit. (Zaire), in *MD*. pp. 357, 362-365; P.K. SARPONG, art. cit. (Ghana), *MD*. p. 542.

[47] RH.6: "through dialogue, contacts, prayer in common, investigation of the treasures of human spirituality...".

[48] RH.11-12; those religions are to be seen as paths for seeking God and for giving a full meaning to human life, as paths permeated by reflections of the one and only Truth and by the "seeds of the Word"; they are a magnificent patrimony of the human spirit.

[49] Cf. *Guidelines for Interreligious Dialogue*, published at Varanasi 1977, quoted by P. ROSSANO, art. cit., pp. 89f; see M. ZAGO O.M.I., *Dialogue in a Buddhist Context*, in *IMC.II* p. 91.

Within the context of that dialogue the concern with Asian spiritualities is growing. The need of prayer and contemplation is ever more felt. Asian traditions of meditation stimulate us to encounter the Lord in prayerful serenity and to rediscover the most suitable ways of opening our hearts to his life-giving Spirit who cries out "Abba!". Thus the Final Statement of the second plenary Assembly of FABC, Calcutta 1978, on "Prayer: the Life of the Church of Asia":

> "The spirituality characteristic of the religions of our continent stresses a deeper awareness of God and the whole self in recollection, silence and prayer, flowering in openness to others, in compassion, non-violence, generosity. Through these and other gifts it can contribute much to our spirituality which, while remaining truly christian, can yet be greatly enriched. Sustained and reflective dialogue with them in prayer ... will reveal to us what the Holy Spirit has taught to express in a marvellous variety of ways".[50]

Chapter three: INCULTURATION: EVANGELIZING ALL MEN, EVERY MAN, THE WHOLE MAN

We have seen that no credible mission of the christian community, no genuine process of inculturation, can remain indifferent to persons and communities of other living faiths and religious traditions.[51] Now we will consider another important sphere of relationships between the faith community and the larger pluralistic society, namely in its secular, socio-economic and political aspects.

---

[50] Cf. FABC Papers n° 13, part. II, *Final Statement and Recommendations*, n. 35 pp. 20 f. See also: A. de NICOLAS SJ, *Formation and Spirituality for Mission,* in *IMC.II* p. 220.

[51] See chapter I. Also P. D'SOUZA, art. cit., in *MD.* p. 25; M.A. ODUYOYE, art. cit., in *MD.* pp. 44-48; J. MUTISO-MBINDA, art. cit., in *MD.* pp. 190-192; R.C. ROSSIGNOL M.E.P., art. cit., in *MD.* pp. 312 f; J.A. DiNOIA O.P., *The Universality of Salvation and the Diversity of Religious Aims,* in *MD.* pp. 337 f; A NAMBIAPARAMBIL C.M.I., art. cit. in *MD.* p. 421; J.B. LIBANIO SJ, *Religious Freedom and the Local Church's Responsibility for Mission. Brazil,* in *MD.* pp. 472 f; P.K. SARPONG, art. cit., in *MD.* p. 539.

Particularly in the Third World the Church is much concerned about the integral human development of society, so that notions like human dignity, equality and fraternity may become a social reality. Whereas traditional Church doctrine has strongly emphasized "man", now we have become clearly aware of the dialectical relationship between "man" and societal "structures". Hence in evangelizing people and in building christian communities we must approach the question from both angles. How are people, human structures and human values affected by life-situations? how is man particularly in his quest of salvation influenced by culture, which is not merely his "milieu" but truly and intimately is part of his self?

Within the perspective of God's kingdom the task of the Church in the world is, on the one hand, to recognize the autonomy of the earthly affairs and the dignity of the human person, and to manifest its solidarity with the entire human family; and on the other, to see to it that we all remain united in Christ and led by the Spirit and have access to the Father.[52] This task of presenting Christ as "the source and model of that renewed humanity penetrated with brotherly love, sincerity and a peaceful spirit, to which all aspire" (AG.8) concerns not only countries or continents different from those of centuries old Christianity. Profound and rapid changes, ever faster social and cultural transformation in these latter areas, have become a permanent situation. Nowadays continuous inculturation of the faith is called for everywhere if we wish the event of the Word to be relevant to modern man and the new subcultural groups. More than ever these "christian" areas need a reinculturation of evangelization.

The "holistic mission" of the Church[53] has been emphasized time and again by the Magisterium: in his apostolic exhortation "Evangelii Nuntiandi" (1975) Paul VI describes evangelization as the endeavour "to transform the hearts of each and every man, along

---

[52] Cf. GS.36 on the rightful autonomy of earthly affairs; see also the description of "Church" (or rather "the followers of Christ") in GS.1.

[53] This term recently in favour is meant to convey that mission fundamentally refers to man in his totality, as whole man. Cf. K. MÜLLER, Holistic Mission oder Das Umfassende Heil, in H. WALDENFELS, Denn Ich bin bei euch, Zürich 1978, pp. 75-83.

18

with their activities, their lives and their whole environment"
(EN.18). John Paul II considers in *"Redemptor Hominis"* as
essential the Church's "solicitude for man, for his humanity, for the
future of men on earth and therefore also the course set for the
whole of development and progress" (RH.15). But he also raises the
critical question — and here the prophetical function of the
christian community in its milieu is touched upon —:

"... is man as man developing and progressing, or is he regressing
and being degraded in his humanity? Is he becoming truly better,
that is to say, more mature spiritually, more aware of the dignity of
his humanity, more responsible, more open to others, especially the
neediest and the weakest, and readier to give and to aid all?"
(ibidem).

More specifically the Asian Colloquium on Ministries (Hong
Kong, February 27 - March 5, 1977) sums up the challenge for the
Church in Asia:

"In *economics*: how to contribute to the eradication of stark poverty,
by an authentic dialogue of life with the poor of Asia, without
fostering materialism. — In *social life*: how to preserve the authentic
values of personalism and family life in the face of urbanization and
technological progress. — In *political matters*: how to help our
people find an Asian style of authentic participative leadership in
government at all levels. — In *cultural matters*: how to find their own
national and Asian identity, by blending ancient and modern values
in face of the future ahead".[54]

While sharing "the joys and the hopes, the griefs and the
anxieties" of all around us, especially the poor and the afflicted
(cf. GS.1), it is good to view our participation as christians in
efforts for development and progress in eschatological perspective,
encompassing the totality of creation, the whole of mankind and
every man, in the spiritual, historical and socio-economic
dimension. Salvation in God's kingdom ultimately consists not

---

[54] Cf. *Conclusions,* Part I.A. Asian Situation at Present, N. 12 on the
situational challenges to the christian Church in Asia, *Asian Colloquium on
Ministries in the Church,* ed. P.S. de Achutegui SJ, Card. Bea Institute for
Ecumenical Studies, Carmelo & Bauermann, Inc., Manila 1977, p. 22.

merely in the survival of the spirit, but means the resurrection of the whole man, and this includes the redemption of the whole social, economic and political relationship of man's earthly life.[55] It is by actual involvement out of wholehearted commitment to the common welfare of our people, that we christians live up and testify to our faith in God who is present in our midst and unceasingly works our salvation now and in the hereafter.

The secularization of society is a phenomenon that continues to emerge all over the world. It has unique characteristics dependent upon the society from which it emerges.[56] Often enough it has proved a stumbling block to the christian community.[57] At times the Church has seen itself as quite apart from the process of modernization, of the emergence and the spread of the secular mind, as if Christianity were merely concerned with "heavenly things". Not seldom the Church has failed to deal effectively with secularization. In more highly technological societies there is often a disparity between the actual daily experience of the people and the way the Gospel message is preached. Sometimes also the clergy seem to live in a world rather different from, if not alien to that of most lay people. It is as though there were two levels of "language" (in the broadest sense of the word), and consequently of understanding: one related to technology and every day life, the other related to spiritual life and faith experience. Given this disparity the Gospel message will lose a good deal of its relevance and hence its transforming power for many people in their daily "secular" life-situations.[58]

The various trends that emerge almost everywhere, and which nowadays are often closely associated with the secularization of society, interact profoundly with the members and the whole

---

[55] Cf. J. SCHÜTTE S.V.D., *Evangelization and Development in the Light of the Conciliar and Post-Conciliar Theology*, in: *Service and Salvation*, ed. J.M. Pathrapankal, Bangalore, T.P.I., 1973, p. 378.

[56] Cf. M.A. ODUYOYE, art. cit., *MD.*, pp. 148-154; J. REILLY SJ art. cit., *MD.* pp. 209 f; O. BOHN, *The Mission of the Local Church and the Inculturation of the Gospel. Denmark, MD.* pp. 491, 493 f.

[57] Cf. J.H. SASAKI, art. cit., *MD.* p. 107; C.T. HALLY S.S.C. art. cit., *MD.* pp. 246 f; P.K. SARPONG, art. cit., *MD.* p. 542; R.J. SCHREITER C.P.P.S., *MD.* p. 550.

[58] Cf. A. PIERIS SJ, art. cit., *MD.* pp. 427, 431 f; O. BOHN, art. cit., *MD.* pp. 490; R.J. SCHREITER C.P.P.S., art. cit., *MD. pp. 544, 552 f.*

atmosphere of the christian community. The prophetic function of witnessing to Gospel values particularly in modernized societies is precisely part of the "secularity" of the faith community.[59] But even for countries with a small christian minority, taking into account the profound changes which are ever more part and parcel of daily experience, it holds true that christians

> "should exert themselves lest modern man, overly intent on the science and technology of today's world, become a stranger to things divine. Rather, let them awaken in him a fiercer yearning for that truth and charity which God has revealed" (AG.11).[60]

Let us take secularization not as a stumbling block or a threat to Christianity, but rather as a challenge to our way of preaching the Gospel and of living our faith; as a "sign of the times" impelling us to rediscover the meaningfulness of the Gospel message and of Gospel values for ourselves and for others; as a unique chance for christian communities to renew themselves by the painstaking and often painful process of inculturation which, however, will become a new source of life and strength for their mission in society.

Political, economics, social structures and trends are — not the least in developing countries — often marked with injustice.[61] Hence justice, liberation from oppression and misery, peace and the wellbeing of the masses need to be our deep concerns today.[62]

---

[59] Cf. T. BALASURIYA O.M.I., art. cit., *MD.* pp. 113 f; 119; J.M. RIVERA-M.R. RAMOS, *The Mission of the Local Church in Secular Society. A Reflection from the Context of the Latin American Church, MD.* pp. 162, 165-168.

[60] It is interesting to note, that e.g., not only in rural areas, but also in the major cities in Indonesia where the modernizing process advances continually, quite a few people (among them also intellectuals) join the various trends of "kebatinan" (movements of "interior life"). The Church certainly has to respond to this desire for spiritual life, particularly in the context of modernization.

[61] Cf. A. MOTANYANE O.M.I., *The Missionary Dimensions of the Local Church. Lesotho, MD.* pp. 79 f; H.H. HERRARA O.P. art. cit., *MD.* pp. 121-138; J.M. RIVERA-M.R. RAMOS, art. cit., *MD.* pp. 155-168; Ph. NKIERE KENA C.I.C.M., art. cit., *MD.* pp. 291 f; J.N.M. WIJANGAARDS M.H.M.-P. DIRVEN M.H.M., art. cit., *MD.* pp. 331, 337, 345; Chr. TAN R.G.S., *The Liberation and Justice Dimension of the Mission of the Local Church, The Philippines, MD.* pp. 618-621.

[62] M.A. ODUYOYE, art. cit., *MD.* pp. 152-154; H.E. WINTER O.M.I., *Catholic, Evangelical, and Reformed: An Ecumenical Strategy for Total Evangelization, MD.* p. 226; B. ASHBY, *The Liberation and Justice Dimension of the Mission of the Local*

There ought to be in our communities an ever deeper commitment, a growing involvement, a continual process of discovery of how to take initiatives and help people around who have fallen victims to injustice and oppression not only on the part of individuals but even more so caused by structures in society. The poor and the deprived, a major — if not the largest — part of the population of Third World countries, totally caught up in their sufferings and struggles, call us to understand deeper and carry out more faithfully Christ's liberative mission.[63] Indeed, the particular emphasis on the option for the poor in various local Churches appears closely related to the process of their inculturation.[64]

Decrees 4 and 5 of the 32d General Congregation inculcate the need of taking sides with our brothers and sisters who amidst their sufferings long for liberation and authentic growth, in order that inculturation be a truly living process. We have to work not only *for* the poor, but — as has been stressed also by our Asian bishops — from the position of the poor and with the poor. The remark may be made that in Asian countries, where religious seekers voluntarily opt to be poor in their search for the Saving Truth — a type of poverty quite different from poverty forced upon people by injustice and oppression, — preaching the Gospel from the perspective of the poor of Yahwe, of that poverty of spirit that prepares us to encounter Christ, may be quite relevant and appealing to many people.[65]

Confronted with the threat of communism, which in Asia among the millions living in extreme poverty stands all chances to become ever more vigorous, BIMA I discerned as one of our

---

Church. *New Zeeland, MD.* pp. 561-563; G. COLLET, *Liberation for Freedom: Reflection on the Task of the Church, MD.* pp. 574-577; M. KEENAN R.S.H.M., *The Liberation and Justice Dimension ... A United States Experience, MD.* pp. 579-595; G. OJO, *Idem ... An African View, MD.* pp. 598-600; Chr. SIDOTI, art. cit., *MD.* pp. 613-615.

[63] Cf. J.M. RIVERA-M.R. RAMOS, art. cit., *MD.* pp. 166 f; A. PIERIS SJ, art. cit. *MD.* pp. 427-428.

[64] Cf. J.M. RIVERA-M.R. RAMOS, art. cit., *MD.* pp. 155-168; A. PIERIS SJ, art. cit., *MD.* pp. 426-441.

[65] Cf. A. PIERIS SJ, *Speaking of the Son of God in Non-Christian Cultures, e.g. in Asia,* Conc. n. 153 (1982) pp. 65-70; also: *A Working Paper on Inculturation,* in: *On Inculturation,* p. 19.

primary tasks "to see the signs of the times as a challenge to find a new synthesis between Gospel and Asian cultures, between Gospel and Asian religions". It urged us to look shead of our time "for the final global attack on the slavery imposed on man by man", and to "understand Christianity as a vital alternative to Marxism in the uncompromising battle for an authentic, i.e. christian liberation of those enslaved, not guided by materialistic ideologies but by the love of Christ".[66] The question "how to make the Servant Church a reality?" is answered by BIMA I with the suggestion to make our institutions "efficient tools for social conscientization and radical social change".[67]

For BISA VI (1983) one of the greatest signs of hope has been the increasing number of "Church people" trying to live "the preferential option for the poor", identifying themselves with the poor in life style and in the struggle for justice and a more human existence. Particularly the proliferation of Basic Christian Communities and Basic Human Communities is seen as a sign of hope that the Church will become the Church of the poor.[68] Through the few from whom inculturation requires identification with those in greatest want the Church will learn "in what culture it is taking flesh and what concrete modality its work of salvation and liberation should assume".[69]

One thing, however, ought to be kept in mind: the commitment to social justice and integral human development may not be divorced from "directly" announcing the Gospel. The task of development should be a function of the total transformation of man by the word of God. Thus humanity will find its way back to God's kingdom.[70] Preaching Christ should remain at the heart of all missionary activity, lest mission work be regarded as a merely humanitarian affair, or even worse: the christian message be rejected as a political interference or cultural aggression.[71]

---

[66] Cf. BIMA I, in *IMC.II*, p. 19.
[67] Cf. BIMA I, in *IMC.II*, p. 27.
[68] Cf. *Reflections at the Conclusion of BISA VI*, ad 1 and 2.
[69] Cf. *A Working Paper on Inculturation*, in: *On Inculturation*, p. 19.
[70] Cf. J. Schütte S.V.D., art. cit., p. 367.
[71] "A sample survey made in India showed that 75% of educated Hindus regarded mission work not as a religious activity but as a humanitarian affair, like that of the Peace Corps' workers", BIMA I, in *IMC.II*, p. 23.

Chapter four: INCULTURATION: MATURING UNTO "THE HEIGHT OF CHRIST'S FULL STATURE" [72]

Setting out from the theological concept of "inculturation" as the realization of the paschal mystery in its trinitarian structure in human society we have considered successively two dimensions of inculturation, namely its relationship with religious values within culture, and with the socio-economic and political aspect of society. Now we will reflect more closely on the process of inculturation.

Taking "culture" in the same sense as it is understood by "*Gaudium et Spes*" *(53)*, "*Evangelii Nuntiandi*" (20), and the final message of the Bishops' Synod of 1977 (n. 5), it is by no means easy to set up universally valid directives, since the process of building christian communities is to take place everywhere in an immensely wide diversity of situations. Numerous are the problems implied in inculturation understood as the experience of christians living in a definite cultural space, inheriting the traditional values of their own culture, yet wishing to be open to other cultures. How are they to accept their own past with discernment and to build up their future with their present resources?

Inculturation touches what is most intimate and sensitive in the human heart. It is not enough just to understand the Gospel. This Word event should become an inexhaustible source of new life. It should induce a continual and ever more radical conversion: sharing the death of Christ, so that day by day we may live a new life in Him. Clearly the message of salvation needs to be transmitted in a style fully in tune with the people's life experiences, therefore in harmony with their cultural setting.

Inculturation also has to do with the social effect of certain Church structures on the communities, but also with the problem of incorporating the "mechanisms" of social communication into the communion of faith. It has to do with the very meaning of liturgical gestures and symbolic expressions, but as much with religious symbols of the people which when purified could be fruitfully integrated in christian worship. It has to do with the very formulation of christian doctrine, it this is to be truly meaningful

---

[72] Cf. Eph. 4,13.

24

for our every day life in very particular circumstances.[73] All this entails that transformation must be continually operative in the christian community, ongoing evangelization, unceasing conversion and renewal day in and day out.[74]

We have already mentioned the three guiding principles proposed by R.J. Schreiter for the dynamics of transformation.[75]

According to the principle of *inclusion*, based on Jesus' invitation to all to become part of God's kingdom, all people and cultures, in principle, can attain their eschatological fulfillment, when placed under Christ's rule; then he will place himself under God who will rule completely over all.[76] Hence the christian community may not too quickly exclude persons, customs, or social relationships.

The principle of *judgment* flows from Jesus' call to conversion needed for the entry into the kingdom. The community may not found its sense of inclusion on cultural romanticism, because culture, while good, is contaminated by sin. The criteria for judgment are not to be drawn from the culture of those who introduce the Gospel. The point is: how the Word event could involve as many people as possible.

The principle of *service* grows out of Jesus' teaching on how to serve others. We must center upon the other, listen to him, enter his reality. Only within this attitude of service can inclusion and judgment be developed properly.

"Without service, inclusion can become a paternalistic gesture ... Without service, judgment can become self-righteous ... Service happens in areas where the hearer's culture needs service, not where the speaker's culture either thinks service is needed, or where it feels more comfortable serving".[77]

---

[73] Cf. A. de NICOLAS SJ, art. cit., in *IMC.II* pp. 219 f.

[74] Cf. J.H. SASAKI, art. cit., *MD.* p. 104; H.H. HARRARA, art. cit., *MD.* pp. 136-138; J.T. BOBERG S.V.D., art. cit., *MD.* p. 234; BOKA DI MPASI LONDI SJ, art. cit., *MD.* pp. 357-360; J.J. KNIGHT S.V.D., art. cit., *MD.* pp. 410 f; O. BOHN, art. cit., *MD.* pp. 491 f; P. DREGO, *The Mission of the Local Church and the Inculturation of the Gospel. India, MD.* pp. 520, 527-529; R.J. SCHREITER C.P.P.S., art. cit., *MD.* pp. 546-548.

[75] See above: chapter II, n. 7, footnote 41.

[76] Cf. 1 Cor. 15, 23-28 on the eschatological meaning of the paschal mystery.

[77] Cf. R.J. SCHREITER C.P.P.S., art. cit., *MD.* pp. 546 f.

Many are the problems encountered along the process of inculturation. Suffice it to mention just a few questions.

Firstly, dialectical tensions will arise, apparent incompatibilities or dilemmas, alternatives to be reconciled in a serene and healthy equilibrium; e.g., between the universal and the contingent, between the desire to maintain identity and the need of purification; between unity and pluralism; between centralization of authority and the principle of subsidiarity; between enlightened paternalism and equality of rights; between boldness and prudence.[78]

Another problem may appear amidst young nations in the wake of their struggle for independence from colonial powers. Exaggerated patriotism with strongly emotional overtones may lead them to overreact against their unhappy past and to absolutize their own cultural values. This may influence christians to the extent of overemphasizing particularities of their local Church and isolating their communities from outside influences. Thus damage may be done, since the local Church only can grow healthily within the communion with other Churches.

Also, meaningful contextual reflections on faith have often been restrained by the resistance among the clergy who tenaciously cling to traditional outdated formulas. Meaningful christian life and faithfulness to tradition supposes readiness to accept the possibility of reformulating christian faith in various cultural terms and of celebrating the mystery of salvation in different rituals and symbols. A dogmatism of word and symbol alienates faith and its expression in prayer and liturgy from every day life. The Gospel will lose its relevance. It will have nothing to say on real actual problems.[79]

The more complete inculturation of the Gospel message may also be hindered, when christian symbols apparently accepted by communities have become a means for the faithful to defend themselves and preserve their cultural identity as a people. These symbols, meant to convey the traditional christian meaning, actually have taken on a different content for those who use them. Behind the symbols traditional religious beliefs and values may still persist inaltered ("unchristianized").[80]

---

[78] Cf. *A Working Paper on Inculturation*, in *On Inculturation*, p. 21.

[79] Cf. A. de Nicolas SJ, art. cit., in *IMC.II*, p. 229.

[80] Cf. J.B. Libanio SJ, art. cit., *MD*. p. 479; C.R. Cadorette M.M., *Christianity and the Aymara — a Case Study, MD*. pp. 500-514.

Inculturation is threatened by a certain liberalism which, in the name of inculturation, would leave out essential elements of christian faith, or accept symbolism and forms of life inconsistent with Gospel values. Along the process of inculturation we should remain faithful to the Gospel to be set forth with all its demands and in all its integrity.[81]

Certain conditions are to be observed, if the inculturation process is to take place in a right and balanced way.

Inculturation is not an abstract encounter between "faith" and "culture", or between two "systems", but a dialogue between groups of people. We are dealing with people of flesh and blood in their real life situations, cultural, religious, social, economic, political. The process of their accepting the Gospel, therefore, should not merely be considered theologically, nor from the point of view of the evangelizer. Account must be taken also of the psychological process of receiving christian faith on the part of the "evangelized", so that the evangelizer knows which approach to take, which attitude to assume.[82]

Inculturation supposes "solidarity of christians to the world, dynamic relationship and interaction with the world, insertion into the historical movement".[83] Basic communities, in order to be genuinely christian and communities at the grassroots level, should be ordained to the service of society and thus embody the servantship of Jesus. They need an "incarnational" approach in carrying out their mission.

Communities living in a pluricultural situation must be docile and sensitive to all values conducive to salvation. They must stay open to cultural value expressions and appearances in the perspective of human fulfilment in God's kingdom. That sensitivity gives shape to their serving mission in concreto. Their ministers

---

[81] The *Working Paper on Inculturation* stresses rejection of compromise as a constant in the Church, referring to Paul's example who refused to mitigate the Gospel in order to please people (cf. 1 Cor. 1,17; 5,7; 9,12; Gal. 1,10; 2,11). *On Inculturation* p. 21.

[82] Cf. M. Amaladoss SJ, art. cit., in *IMC.II*, p. 35; J. Tong, *"Evangelization" as seen from the Chinese Viewpoint*, quoting Mr. Lee Chis-sung with his six models (types of psychological processes) of Chinese people receiving christian faith, in *IMC.II*, pp. 2 f.

[83] Cf. D.S. Amalorpavadass, art. cit., *IMC.II*, pp. 202 f.

must do away with prejudices resulting from a concrete historically conditioned human and spiritual education, persisting in an unconscious way, but real enough to block understanding of the people and to damage the inculturation process.[84] Then dialogue becomes really the key of missionary activity,

> "a witnessing to Christ in word and deed, by reaching out to people in the concrete reality of their daily lives, in their particular cultural context, their own religious traditions, their socio-economic conditions".[85]
> "the ideal form of evangelization, where in humility and mutual support we seek together with our brothers and sisters that fullness of Christ, which is God's plan for the whole of creation, in its entirety and its great and wonderful diversity".[86]

R.J. Schreiter C.P.P.S. suggests an assumption and two criteria for evaluating the inculturation process.

The assumption: since evangelization means "the transformation of the human and social situation toward the kingdom of God", the inculturated Word of God must always address the central values that give form to a culture.

The criterion of *affirming the identity of the culture* based on the theology of creation: if God found the world good, then there must be much to affirm in a local situation; also on the theology of incarnation: if God revealed himself in the person of Jesus, and his message was meant for all cultures, then any cultural setting has more positive than negative qualities. Therefore: a) the local Church should not hastily have value and identity forms in the culture changed; b) the Church should help keep in mind the crucial role of the sense of identity (inner consistency and continuity) for a community, so that amidst innovations it maintains a point of reference; c) this criterion is linked with the inclusive character of God's kingdom which cannot attain its fullness until it has transformed each human culture and situation.[87]

---

[84] Cf. A. de NICOLAS SJ, art. cit., *IMC.II*, p. 227.

[85] Cf. *A Letter from the Participants* (of **BIMA** I) *to the Bishops of Asia*, sub 5, *IMC.II*, p. 28.

[86] Cf. *A Letter...*, sub 10, *IMC.II*, p. 29.

[87] Cf. the guiding principles of *inclusion*, n. 15.

The criterion of *locating the need for social change* based on the theology of redemption.[88] Situations are in need of transformation, of passing through death and resurrection in Jesus Christ. To be noted: a) by looking at points of social change and the previous response of religious activity to them, we can find the deeper needs for change in the community, the ways toward solution ordinarily taken, the range and flexibility of response within that community facing changes; b) locating the need for social change can open up the community more effectively to its environment; the adequacy of a community's response is tested while confronted with larger social, economic, and political realities with which the community is to come to terms; c) effective inculturation not only means identifying points of stress or ill in the community, but also identifying pseudo-solutions of those problems; real solutions address the root of problems; often pseudo-solutions become enshrined in a culture because people feel helpless in dealing with enormous problems.

"Both criteria are mutually related. Identity is not a static reality; change is part of living. Social change without some point of reference leads to alienation and inner death. Without identity, a community loses its soul; without facing change, it loses contact with the larger world of which it is part. Theologically they represent the two dimensions by which we experience God: creation and redemption".[89]

Chapter five: INCULTURATION: ACTUALIZING CHRIST'S MISSION AS A COMMUNITY OF FAITH

In the previous chapters we have considered successively the theological concept of "inculturation", its realization in the dimension of religious values and with regard to socio-economic and political life in society, and the process of inculturation in christian communities.

In the following pages we further elaborate on the christian community as subject or agent of inculturation, reflecting in

---

[88] We would say: based on the paschal mystery. See also the guiding principle of *judgment*, n. 15.

[89] Cf. R.J. SCHREITER C.P.P.S., art. cit., *MD*. pp. 548-550.

successive sections on the role of the community in general, on the small christian communities more particularly, on the role of lay people, of lay leaders of the community, and finally on the role of ordained ministers.

Section I: The Role of the Community in General

Inculturation is not the work of an elite or of leaders who create a new way of living christian faith in their "laboratory", and then communicate it to the people. Experts and leaders certainly play an important part, the role of facilitation. The primary agent of inculturation, however, is the christian community. The subjects in the process are the people themselves.

The deeper levels of "inculturation" of the Gospel can be realized only from within the community, through a continuous process by which christians renew themselves and confront the various aspects of their cultural heritage with the Word of God in such a way that these values are transformed and incorporated into the authentic faith expression of the community.[90] There is no better point of reference for effective inculturation than "the mass of ordinary people, with their traditions, their ancestral wisdom, their intuitions, their sensibilities and apprehensions, which have developed certain forms of expression over the centuries".[91] The apriorism of laboratory inculturation, without contact with concrete reality, may even endanger the whole process of inculturation.

> "Evangelization loses much of its force and effectiveness, if it does not take into consideration the actual people to whom it is addressed, nor use their language, their signs and symbols, nor answer the questions they ask; and if it does not have an impact on their concrete life" (EN.63).

---

[90] On this ongoing self-evangelization and renewal within the community as the foundation of mission, cf. P.A. BIEN-AIMÉ O.P., art. cit., *MD*. pp. 11 f; P. D'SOUZA, art. cit., *MD*. p. 27; J.H. SASAKI art. cit., *MD*. p. 101; J. REILLY SJ, art. cit., *MD*. p. 206; H.E. WINTER O.M.I., art. cit., *MD*. pp. 216, 221 f; A. PIERIS SJ, art. cit., *MD*. pp. 438 f; O. BOHN, art. cit., *MD*. p. 490; R.J. SCHREITER C.P.P.S., art. cit., *MD*. pp. 549 f.

[91] Cf. *A Working Paper on Inculturation*, in *On Inculturation*, p. 13.

Hence efforts should be taken at deepening ever more the faith of the christian community, at helping christians live their faith "realistically" and see its relevance in today's life situations. Their minds are to be open to what actually is happening in society, to "the signs of the times". They are to involve themselves deeply in corresponsibility, in shaping the future of their homeland. A new mentality is required in order to change structures of society and patterns of life obstructive to integral human development in the christian sense.

Section II: The Role of small Christian Communities

In small christian communities the Spirit of the risen Lord is present, making his death and resurrection manifest and operative in society. These communities are expected to help restore the community of all men by breaking down barriers, destroying hostility, reconciling people, realizing communion and promoting human brotherhood.[92]

Since these are communities springing up at grassroots levels, we can only facilitate their emergence and animate their growth. When they do come up, we can recognize and encourage them so as not to become closed groups or elitist cliques but open human and christian communities, inserted in their milieu, serving society, reaching out in common projects of apostolate and common witness of life.[93] There, indeed, we come to grips with the complexity of their cultural situation. The bishops of the young Churches have taken note of their importance in the process of inculturation and have made certain suggestions in the Synod on Evangelization (1974) and on Catechesis (1977).[94].

Much, of course, remains to be done about many traditional communities composed of "practising-consuming", generally rather passive members. The ideal is to foster communities which hold Christ as the ultimate norm while facing challenges and choices,

---

[92] Cf. D.S. AMALORPAVADASS, art. cit., *IMC.II*, pp. 203 f.

[93] Cf. D.S. AMALORPAVADASS, art. cit., p. 206.

[94] M. ZAGO refers to his article: *Communauté et évangélization. Orientations des Synodes de 1974 et 1977 et prospectives missionnaires*, Omnis Terra, french edition, june 1979; see art. cit., *IMC.II*, pp. 95, 100.

while reflecting on their own experiences and discerning ways of life and apostolate; communities continually strengthened by faith and confirmed by ongoing self-evangelization, with the encounter between life situations and the Word of God at its heart;[95] communities nourished by their life of prayer and worship, important elements of apostolate amidst the religious quest of Asia;[96] communities in communion with other communities, but also open to the expectations and to the life of the people, to the present and the emerging cultural values. Such communities

> "can hope to discern, in the Spirit, how to understand the aspirations and values of their brothers who share with them the same culture but not the same faith ... to discover the way of witnessing to Christ among them and to make the values of the Kingdom already present or still lacking growth in their midst".[97]

The ecclesial reality and the experience of Christ will be all the more authentic if based on the genuine human experience of communities, where every thing is person-oriented without excluding task-orientation, where there is deep inter-personal relationship, a sense of real belonging, an all-round sharing, a dynamic outreach to respond to persons and situations in the milieu.[98]

However, there could be in such communities a tendency towards self-enclosure, particularism, isolationism. Hence it is

---

[95] Cf. P.A. BIEN-AIMÉ O.P., art. cit., *MD.*, p. 12; J.H. SASAKI, art. cit., *MD.* pp. 101 f; H.H. HERRARA O.P., art. cit., *MD.* pp. 127-133; L. BOSETO, art. cit., *MD.* p. 184; C.T. HALLY S.S.C., art. cit., *MD.* p. 262; J.N.M. WIJNGAARDS M.H.M., P. DIRVEN M.H.M., art. cit., *MD.* p. 345; F.F. CLAVER SJ, *Religious Freedom and the Local Church's Responsibility for Mission. The Philippines, MD.* pp. 453 f; A. NAMBIAPARAMBIL C.M.I., art. cit., *MD.* pp. 418f; A. PIERIS SJ, art. cit., *MD.* pp. 431 f; P.K. SARPONG, art. cit., *MD.* P. 542; M. KEENAN R.S.H.M., art. cit., *MD.* pp. 593 f.

[96] See: The Second Plenary Assembly of FABC *Prayer — the Life of the Church of Asia,* Part. II. *Final Statement and Recommendations,* n. 28; n. 29: "All aspects of the Christian community's prayer should be renewed ... Because of their special relevance to the present Asian scene, however, we have discussed more fully some means which can help foster Christian prayer and witness in our countries. These are: inculturation, interreligious dialogue, and the renewed formation in prayer of all in the ranks of the People of God...", FABC Papers n° 13 p. 19.

[97] Cf. M. ZAGO O.M.I., art. cit., *IMC.II,* pp. 95 f.

[98] Cf. D.S. AMALORPAVADASS, art. cit., *IMC.II,* pp. 205 f.

important to remain within the communion of the universal Church, to whose role it belongs to promote intercultural exchange and coordination in such a way that the many cultural expressions converge towards a unity of faith in mutual sharing and service.

Section III: The Role of the Lay People

We have moved far off from the mentality expressed in the schema of Vatican I:

> "The Church of Christ is not a community of equals in which all the faithful have the same rights. It is a society of unequals, not only because among the faithful some are clerics and some are laymen, but particularly because there is in the Church the power from God whereby to some it is given to sanctify, teach and govern, and to others not".[99]

The same theological climate still appeared in Pius X's encyclical "*Vehementer nos*" (1906):

> "The college of pastors alone has the right and the authority to lead and guide all the members toward the goal of the community. The majority have no other right but to let themselves be led, and follow the shepherds like an obedient flock".[100]

This amounts to saying that, while the clergy took care of the Church, the world was the lay persons' area of responsibility under the guidance of the clergy.

Theologically Vatican II means an ecclesiological breakthrough for the laity, where it teaches that the People of God share a common dignity from their rebirth in Christ, the same filial grace and the same vocation to perfection.

> "Hence, there is in Christ and in the Church no inequality on the basis of race or nationality, social condition or sex..." (LG.32).

---

[99] Cf. the first draft of the *Constitution on the Church of Christ* of Vatican I (1870), chapt. X, J. NEUNER and H. ROOS, *The Teaching of the Catholic Church*, ed. by K. RAHNER SJ, New York 1966, n° 369 pp. 219 f.

[100] Quoted by J.M. de MESA, *The Participation of Lay Men and Lay Women in the Decisions of the Church as Ministry*, in *IMC.II*, pp. 161, 177.

The consciousness is growing of the necessary contribution to be made by the laity in corresponsibility for the community. The continued dominance of clerical control is recognized as an impediment to the community's full development.[101] Not only are the laity truly coresponsible for the Church's mission in society (cf. AA.2). If their presence is not felt, then the christian community cannot be considered truly established or fully alive, because

"the Gospel cannot be deeply imprinted on the talents, life and work of any people without the active presence of laymen" (AG.21).

The Church, therefore, insists on attention to be paid "to raising up a mature Christian laity" even in the very founding of a Church (ibidem).

But while full participation of the laity is confirmed by conciliar ecclesiology, and they are encouraged to be involved in the life of the Church and to participate actively in the decisions of society,[102] "*Apostolicam Actuositatem*", specifically dedicated to the laity, does not even touch upon their participation in the decisions of the Church. The question is put forward, whether we could not go further then to their taking part in the decision-making *process* (by just offering advice, suggestions, recommendations). Why should not there be a communality of decision *making* itself,[103] particularly when this concerns the christian communities' mission in secular society? Why does not the fundamental collegiality and correspondsibility of the one People of God come through?[104]

AA.10 seems to provide an exception relevant to our theme on inculturation:

"The laity should accustom themselves to working in the parish in close union with their priests, bringing to the church community their own and the world's problems as well as questions concerning human salvation, all of which should be *examined and resolved by common deliberation*".[105]

---

[101] Cf. P.A. BIEN-AIMÉ O.P., art. cit., *MD*. pp. 9-21; J.H. SASAKI, art. cit., *MD*. p. 101; J.B. LIBANIO SJ, art. cit., *MD*. pp. 474 f; G. OJO, art. cit., *MD*. pp. 598 f.

[102] Cf. among others: GS.31, 43, 65, 68, 75.

[103] Cf. J.M. de MESA, art. cit., *IMC.II*, pp. 165 f.

[104] Cf. Mrs. Theodore O. WEDEL, *A Response to "Apostolicam Actuositatem"*, in W.M. ABBOTT SJ-J. GALLAGHER, *The Documents of Vatican II*, p. 524.

[105] The underlining is ours. A good illustration is provided by the Council of

Section IV: The Role of Lay Leaders of the Community

In small communities ministries emerge, when the needs of the communities and of their neighbourhood as well as their charism are identified. More and more they rely on their own resources and gradually become well equipped. There will be a variety of ministries, a diversity of functions for a unified purpose (cf. LG.32). Clergy and lay leaders may constitute a "ministerial college". The role of ministries conferred by ordination — the core of the whole "ministerial college" — would have to be rethought according to the original Augustinian idea of incorporation into the "ordo" of the Church ministry.[106]

Parallel to the growing consciousness of communities to become ever better inculturated, there is also an increasing awareness of their ministers of the need to become more and more community based and community oriented, men among men, blessed with certain gifts of the Spirit to be of service to their community. Community and culture are closely linked. The advantage of having leaders coming from the midst of the community is, that they have assimilated basic cultural elements in a natural manner and thus are able to express christian faith and render service in relevant forms. A disadvantage, however, could be, that they may be too deeply involved in the affairs of the community, so that they might take sides with one group against another.

The task of the leaders is to create the atmosphere of freedom and trust, and facilitate the emergence of the creative forces of the community; "to give guidance and to coordinate efforts rather than to initiate and to enforce", to give expression to the sense of faith ("*sensus fidei*") while directing in the Spirit their community.[107]

The FABC sponsored "Asian Colloquium on Ministries in the Church", Hong Kong 1977, mentions that "basic Christian

---

the Laity established by Pope Paul VI in 1967 within the Roman Curia, and later on in 1967 raised to a permanent status as the Pontifical Council of the Laity, of which the majority of the members are lay people.

[106] See P. FRANSEN SJ, *Orders and Ordination*, in: *Sacramentum Mundi*, p. 1146.

[107] Cf. M. AMALADOSS SJ, art. cit., in *IMC.II*, pp. 43 f.

communities are raising questions about leadership styles in the Church". In view of this "bishops and priests must learn to listen to the voice of their people". Indeed, "the local Christian community leaders have also to develop a style of leadership that fits the culture, attitudes and values of their local situation". Our era challenges all of us, the whole People of God, "to be more fully involved, more participative, more outward looking, more responsive and more self-giving, thereby bringing about a style of leadership that underscores genuine corresponsibility".[108]

Important, therefore, is also the formation of lay leaders. While intimately immersed in their own culture, well acquainted with its richnesses and its weaknesses, rich of lived experiences of contact with their own people, they ought to understand the prophetic role as the Church's mission in society, and know well what to expect from christian faith in their cultural situation.[109]

We are to assist particularly those who have a role to play in society in various fields, economic, social, political, cultural. Acting out of their personal responsibility they have as christians to draw their inspiration from the Gospel.

Section V: The Role of Ordained Ministers

The hierarchy, i.e. the Pope at the world level and the bishops at the diocesan level, and the priests — as cooperators dependent on and united with the episcopal order (cf. LG.28) — participatively at lower levels, preside over the communion of christians in *faith* to be lived meaningfully in concrete life situations, to be ever more deepened while in continuity of Christ's mission they respond to the "signs of the times", to become ever more mature while they are creatively and prophetically involved in the transformation of society in its cultural, socio-economic, political and religious dimensions. The hierarchy functions as the bond of *charity*, discerning the many charisms of the Spirit in the communities,

---

[108] *Conclusions*, Part. II, Context of ministries, n. 46, in: P.S. de ACHUTEGUI SJ ed., *Asian Colloquium on Ministries in the Church*, Manila: Federation of Asian Bishops' Conferences, 1977, pp. 33 f; Part IV, Implications for the life and structure of the Church, n. 116, p. 52.

[109] Cf. M. AMALADOSS SJ, art. cit., in *IMVC.II*, p. 43.

providing opportunities for them to grow and to flourish in mutual concord and harmony within the one mystical Body of Christ, directing them towards service to the needs of humanity and its aspirations for a better world.

The hierarchy, therefore, performs its "*diakonia*" to the People of God in all round collegiality, coresponsibility and subsidiarity. In this light the right approach in presiding over the universal communion of faith would be to recognize the autonomy of the regional and/or national hierarchies which can not only divide and demarcate regions, but also recognize new forms of ecclesial communities (e.g., small or "basic" Christian communities, functional groups and centres other than the traditional parishes, etc.) by using better criteria than merely the territorial basis, namely: how the life of faith can best be deepened, how the communion of faith can best be consolidated, how christians or groups of christians can best be or service to society.

Attending to the needs of christians and society at large, it seems but reasonable that local Churches have the right and obligation to determine which ministries are necessary (liturgy, catechesis, social involvement, etc), who are to render these services (ample opportunity should be given to lay people). While these ministries are developing everywhere in christian communities, it is necessary to rethink what would be the task of the priest in concreto; how he would relate to lay ministers or lay leaders in his community; how he would coordinate their ministries and services; which part he would give them in terms of decision making; which exactly is his role, when members of his community are actively involved in cultural life, in social or economic affairs, in politics. When the laity have a right and duty to lead in many secular issues, which is the position of the priest as leader of the community? When the christian community as a whole is the primary agent or subject of inculturation, what exactly is the role of the priest?

Whatever concrete role the priest has to play in the process of inculturating christian faith, it is clear that he should develop certain attitudes of mind: a unifying vision of Salvation history; docility to the Spirit demanding a continuous and attentive listening in prayer; an attitude of discernment ruled by evangelical principles; objective authenticity leading to interior humility; persevering patience and "discreta caritas"; and above all: "*sentire cum Ecclesia*".[110] He needs "a human and spiritual sense of life, touching the most elementary realities of peoples' life"; he needs "to be close and sensitive to their culture, their celebrations, the symbols in which they communicate ... their most cherished values, traditions and insights"; he needs to be "in continuous touch with the concrete events and vicissitudes" of the people. His mission requires a keen sense of the living Mystery of the God of salvation, demanding familiarity with contemplation and prayer.[111]

Yogyakarta, June 10th, 1983, on the feastday of the Sacred Heart of Jesus.

ROBERT HARDAWIRYANA, S.J.

---

[110] Cf. P. ARRUPE SJ, *On Inculturation*, pp. 5 f.
[111] Cf. A. de NICOLAS SJ, art. cit., in *IMC.II*, pp. 234-236.

Arul M. Varaprasadam, S.J.

INCULTURATION: THE CRUCIAL CHALLENGES IN THE INDIAN SITUATION

The estimated population of India, as of January 1985, was 740 million. Although smaller in surface area than China, with a population 250 million less than China's, India, not China, is generally referred to as a subcontinent. The reasons are obvious: India is a mosaic of races and religions, of cultures and languages. India presents a kaleidoscopic picture to a degree few countries in the world do. India is a melting pot of six main races: the Negritos, the broad-headed Negroids of Africa; the Austrics either from Indo-China or from the Mediterranean plain; the Dravidians from Asia Minor; the Brachycephalic, the broad-headed tribes of the Alpine and the Dinaric variety; the Mongoloids; the Nordic Aryans.

The percentages of various religionists are computed as follows: Hindus 76, Muslims 11, Tribal religionists 5, Christians 3, Sikhs 2, Buddhists, Jains ... and persons without religion put together 3.

There is, indeed, what may be termed a mainstream of Indian culture; yet, there are significant differences among the cultures of the Indian peoples, broadly coinciding with the linguistic regions. The Indian Constitution recognises 15 languages officially; there are 700-odd dialects spoken by small groups across the country.

This paper purports to spell out the crucial challenges which emerge in the encounter between the local Christian communities and their traditional cultures: in other words, the interaction between the faith in Jesus Christ received from missionaries and the salient features of the cultures which have shaped the people down the centuries. It aims, likewise, to outline the fruitful possibilities of the encounter.

A CLARIFICATION

The basic assumptions of the concept of Inculturation are taken for granted: namely,

1) that the local Christian community, not the missionary (Indian or non-Indian) who brought the Gospel, is the real agent of Inculturation,

2) that Inculturation, never to be coinceved as a finished product, is essentially a process through which Faith in Jesus endures as the principle of inspiration and of action within a given culture,

3) that a holistic concept of Inculturation presupposes a comprehensive concept of culture, including in its purview the economic, sociopolitical as well as religious dimensions of society at large; and hence that Inculturation of the Faith goes beyond the frontiers of Liturgy, spiritual-pastoral life and ecclesial organisations, and embraces the entire ambit of human life,

4) that Inculturation is basically a challenge to the local Cristian community to tend towards the Freedom of the children of God, having experienced Him in Christ and in the communion with the Universal Church,

5) that thus Evangelization and Inculturation are positively correlated terms in an eminent degree.

QUITE A VARIETY OF INDIAN CHURCHES

The Catholic Christian communities of India may be fitted into six groups:

1) The most ancient group in the country, concentrated in the south-western state of Kerala, but found in sizable numbers in all walks of life throughout India, claiming origin from the Apostle Thomas, and hence known as 'Thomas Christians'. With reference to the origin of their rite they are also known as 'Syrian Christians'.

2) The Konkan or West-Coast Catholics of Mangalore, Goa and Bombay: a significant number of this group is found in the executive posts of the private sector, and in other professions all over India.

3) The Latin-rite Catholics of South India who have emerged in three different waves:

a) Some fisherfolk in Tamilnadu along the Coromandel Coast (known as the Fishery Coast in Portuguese literature) and similar groups in Kerala whose forbears were baptised by the Portuguese missionaries, St Francis Xavier and others from 1536 onwards,

b) Small groups of Christians in Tamilnadu, Andhra and Karnataka, descendants of people who had been converted from the time of Roberto de Nobili (1606-56).

c) Bigger sections belonging largely to the so-called 'low' castes, baptised in the three States mentioned above in the 19th and the 20th centuries by the Paris and Milan foreign missionaries, the Carmelites and the Jesuits.

4) The descendants of the converts in North India through the missionary efforts of the Capuchins.

5) Hundreds of thousands of Adivasis (= original inhabitants) in the Chota-Nagpur plateau of Bihar, Madhya Pradesh and West Bengal, as also in Orissa — converts in the 19th and the 20th centuries through Jesuits and Divine Word missionaries.

6) The Tribals of the North-Eastern States whose conversion was begun in this century by the Passionists and has been continued by the Salesians.

Varying Foci of Inculturation

It is obvious from the above classification that the challenges of inculturation will differ according to the cultures and traditions of the local Christian communities. Though it retains certain contours of meaning, the label 'Indian culture' can become an elusive term as well. Far from being identified with an elitist and classicist culture, it must be seen as a shroud for a host of sub-cultures with different layers within each of them. In other words, one should give up the instinctual impulse to identify Indian culture with the ancient Brahmanical culture which has been dominant for centuries in India. The problems and opportunities engendered by the encounter between the Faith and the particular local culture make up the texture of the challenges presented to the local Christian community.

The Stigma of Foreignness

We may, however, indicate a common trait in the challenges met with by all the Christian communities. It mainly stems from the historical fact that most of these communities have come into being during the period of political and colonial domination by the West. Whether or not the domination positively aided the formation of those communities is not always seriously examined by all non-Christian critics. On the other hand, large sections of the

43

Christian communities do not seriously reflect to see that the cultural appendages of their Faith can indeed be jettisoned without detriment to its integrity. There is no gainsaying the fact that it is a delicate task to disentangle the purely cultural elements from the Faith imbedded in them. The result is that in varying degrees the life-style, theological expression, mode of worship and approach to the Divine Mystery reveal imported features in the Indian Christian communities.

There is thus a subtle, and not so subtle accusation of extra-territorial allegiance directed at the communities of Christians by many of their non-Christian brethren. Two factors would seem to be responsible for this: one, the structures of a highly centralised authority in the Catholic Church with regard to interpretation of the Faith and administration in general. Two, the heavy dependence in finances on the Vatican by the Indian Churches for the training and maintenance of their personnel as well as for the expansion of their physical facilities. One can look down with disdein on dependent Churches, saying that they are manipulated by strings from elsewhere and that 'he who pays the piper calls the tune'. The stigma of foreignness is indeed one dimension in the evaluation of the Indian Churches.

ASIAN DISCOVERY OF A DISTANT MOVEMENT

If the word is a neologism, Inculturation as a process has been followed right from the beginning of Christianity by the disciples who adopted the Way: "So radical indeed was the Inculturation of the New Testament Church that the Jewish Christian communities of Palestine were long regarded by their Jewish contemporaries as a sect (hairesis) of the Jews (Acts 24:5,14;28:2)".[1]

Of the Greek Christians the early second-century *Letter to Diognetus* says: "Christians are not distinguished from the rest of mankind by either country, speech or customs; the fact is they nowhere settle in cities of their own; they use no peculiar language; they cultivate no eccentric mode of life".[2]

---

[1] George Soares PRABHU, "The New Testament As A Model Of Communication", in Samuel RAYAN (Ed.) *The Living Christ* (Incarnation Now), JEEVADHARA 33, May-June 1976, Theology Centre, Alleppey 688 001, Kerala, India, pp. 280-81.

[2] *Letter To Diognetus* 5, translated by J.A. KLEIST in *Ancient Christian Writers* 6 (Westminster: Newman Press, 1948), p. 138.

44

If in the early centuries of Christianity inculturation proved to be so easy and natural within the Mediterranean world, after the lapse of about fifteen centuries it did pose a problem to the Gospel-bearers as well as to the human communities responding to the call of the Gospel. For the very success of inculturation in West Asia and in Europe, deep and enduring as it was, tended to identify the message with the medium. The Hispano-Portuguese attire of the Gospel was an unrelenting obstacle to the heroic efforts at inculturation of a Matteo Ricci in China and of a Roberto de Nobili in India in the 16th century. Local Christian communities seemed to have settled down acquiescing to the foreign garb of the Faith, when at long last, at the turn of the 19th century a new thinking was set in motion in the Asian Churches. Brahmabandhab Upadhyay, Johanns, Dandoy, Raimondo Panikkar, Jules Monchanin, Swami Abhishiktananda, Ignatius Hirudayam and Bede Griffiths may be mentioned as renowned pioneers in the process of inculturation.

The entire gamut of the areas of inculturation is succinctly summed up in the 1974 Statement of the Asian Bishops; "The local Church is a Church incarnate in a people, a Church indigenous and inculturated. And this means concretely a Church in continuous, humble and loving dialogue with the living traditions, the cultures, the religions- in brief, with all the life-realities of the people in whose midst it has sunk its roots deeply and whose history and life it gladly makes its own".[3]

THE INDIAN CHURCHES vis-a-vis THE CHALLENGES OF INCULTURATION

The challenges which inculturation poses to the Indian Churches may be grouped under three heads: 1) Interiority, 2) Word and Worship, 3) A Humanity based on Justice.

1) INTERIORITY: A RESPONSE THROUGH INCULTURATION?

The Indian peoples have been idealized by transient visitors to the country as peoples 'intoxicated by God'. Or expressed more

---

[3] Statement of the Federation of Asian Bishops' Conference, April 1974, pp. 20-21.

soberly, they have been pictured as a people imbued with religiosity. Now, religiosity may be described as a persistent perception of the influence of the supernatural in the numerous daily activities of human beings. Within limits religiosity does retain a certain validity. But as an unwarranted seeking of explanation for natural phenomena from Religion as such, it is a remnant of the pre-scientific age.

In the Indian ethos religiosity would seem to bridge the hiatus between Religion and Morality. But in fact it does not. "Orthodox Hindu religiosity tends to lack genuine humanizing power. True, Hinduism enjoins injunctions and taboos in regard to individual and social life. But the moral law (dharma) is generally assimilated to the cosmic law (rita). The performance of the duties inherent in one's caste (jati-dharma), clan (kula-dharma) and individual avocation (svadharma) is meant to ensure the harmonious functioning of the cosmos. To be moral in this context means conformity to tradition".[4]

Accepting whatever is precious in the spirit of religiosity and sensing indeed the pervasive presence of God in the cosmic order, Christian faith should be challenged and impelled to question all that is inhuman in the cosmos today. In fact it is an imperative of the Faith to de-sacralize to initiate a process of combat against the tendency to accept uncritically the so-called harmonious functioning of the cosmos, the established order, which is often enough the established dis-order. Religiosity leading to interiority will rather provoke the local Christian community to attempt establishing networks of human relationships based on the immanence of God in individuals and in groups of human persons.

Phenomena linked with Religiosity:

Religious Revivalism is one of them. It is a fairly recent phenomenon sweeping over the sub-continent. It is largely a recrudescence rather than a renewal of Religion. Publicity is of the very essence of revivalism: in the name of religion hymns and messages blare through loud-speakers not infrequently causing tension among peoples of different religions. Building of temples

---

[4] Sebastian KAPPEN, *Jesus And Cultural Revolution* (An Asian Perspective) A Build Publication, Bombay 400 050, 1984, p. 62.

46

and mosques, churches and gurdwaras (holy places of Sikhs) goes apace, not to speak of the mushrooming of wayside shrines. The priestly classes of all religions find it lucrative to multiply pilgrim-shrines under the plausible pretext of developing devotion. While refusing to uphold an abstract spirituality, a genuine inculturation will not yield to the craze of a meaningless externalisation of Religion. Rather will it invite the Christian community to evaluate the impact of God's presence within the individual hearts and in society as such. It will likewise draw the attention of the devotees to the negative correlation patent today between religious practices and justice-morality.

Fundamentalism may be viewed as a narrow expression of native religiosity linked with petty nationalism. Iran leading the list, Pakistan and Bangladesh have swarms of fundamentalists. Within Hinduism Rashtriya Swayam Sevak Sangh (= National Self Service Society) is assuming an agressive posture with the intent of turning India into a Hindu State. In this context the challenge to people of any Faith whatever would be the promotion of true secularist values and, at the same time, an appreciation of the authentic values of every individual religion.

This challenge is spelt out for Christians in the Vatican Declaration on the Relationship of the Church to non-Christian Religions (No. 2): "The Church therefore has this exhortation for her sons: prudently and lovingly, through dialogue and collaboration with the followers of other religions, and in witness to Christian faith and life, acknowledge, preserve and promote the spiritual and moral goods found among these men, as well as the values in their society and culture". A French missionary who has delved deep into the spiritual treasures of Hinduism makes a pertinent comment: "It is impossible to minimise the boldness of such a statement. Translated in actual and concrete terms, it means simply that Christians are exhorted, in collaboration with Hindu believers, to preserve and promote the spiritual goods contained in Hindu tradition".[5]

Beyond its popular manifestations, which might be tainted with errors and superstitions, as in any other religion, Hinduism offers

---

[5] Swami ABHISHIKTANANDA, *The Church In India*, Christian Literature Society, Madras 600003, India, p. 77.

an invitation as well as a challenge to interiority. An Indian theologian writes: "We can justifiably wonder whether the experience of interiority and oneness (advaita) so characteristic of Indian religious tradition would really have been possible in the background of Biblical experience. All the same these two experiences are not contradictory but complementary, and mutually enrich our collective consciousness of the divine mystery. It is also conceivable that the same individual or group is not able to enjoy both types of experience equally".[6]

Possibly the most profound challenge to an Indian Christian's aspiration to union with God comes from the 'advaita' (literally 'non-duality', but positively 'oneness'), a basic tenet of Hindu ontology and mysticism, negating all division between the 'Paramatma' (the Great Soul(and the 'Jivatma' (the individual soul in life on earth). And the Christian may be spurred to meet the challenge in an enlightened understanding and assimilation of Christ's 'Priestly Prayer' as given in chapter 17 of John's Gospel.

A Britisher who has grasped the perennial quest of India has this to say regarding the part inculturated Christians have to play in the country: "A spiritual renewal of India, even if inspired or finally assumed by Christian faith, cannot but come from the deep layers of the Hindu mind and spirit. Hence the need for Christians, and especially for those among them who want to prepare the Christian future of India, to plunge deeply into Hindu spiritual experience in order to make it possible for it to be transformed and assumed by Christ, in Christ".[7]

WORD and WORSHIP

The Word of God has long been kept in captive formulation in Greek philosophical terminology. There is a longing in the young Churches today to savour the Word in their own idiom, so that it become a more wholesome nourishment to them. Pluralism in theological expression is indeed fraught with the danger of deviations. As an Indian theologian puts it: "There is a risk here,

---

[6] Michael AMALADOSS, "Inculturation: Theological Perspectives", in *The Living Christ,* op. cit., p. 301.

[7] C. Murray ROGERS, in *The Church In India,* op. cit., Back Cover.

48

both in the incarnation of the faith and in its pluralist expressions. But the risk has to be taken. It is not essentially different from the risk God took in the incarnation of the Word into a small Semitic tribe, in enclosing his message in human languages, in entrusting his memory to a group of very imperfect men. A faith or Church which does not grow from seed or sapling, which does not pass through the risks and pains of growing up, but is ready-made and imported, is likely to remain static and sterile. That precisely is what has happened to many a Church in Asia and in India for full four centuries and more".[8]

There is, fortunately, a felicitous growth in theological sharing through dialogues, symposia and publications. Some of these are surely rooted in the soil, and they reflect the concerns of the struggling Church in a struggling India. We could, however, wish for a more fraternal dialogue between the Bishops and the theologians, so that the people of God, far from being confused, are helped in their involvement in and commitment to the right shaping of the country's future.

Inculturation seems to run into difficulties in the day-to-day expression of Worship. The Church has officially enunciated her norms for adapting the Liturgy to the genius and tradition of different peoples: we have them in numbers 37 to 40 of the Constitution on the Sacred Liturgy of Vatican II. It may be that in some parts of the world the directives of the Church are easily assimilable. But they have created a division within the Catholic communities in India.

It is in the appropriation of Symbols characteristic to the Indian worshipper that controversies have risen. Symbolism itself has a strong grip on the Indian psyche. An Indian writer describes the situation of the early 60s: "India has an 'anima naturaliter liturgica' (a soul naturally liturgical) inclined to worship God in symbol. The complaint of liturgists (and even of psychiatrists) in the West, that one of their greatest difficulties is that people have lost the sense of symbol, that they do not see beyond the obvious reality, and live confined in the present world, could not be made about us. Even the most sophisticated and Westernized of our citizens still respond to symbolism; they celebrate symbolic feasts and are

---

[8] Samuel RAYAN, "Flesh of India's Flesh", in *The Living Christ,* op. cit., p. 263.

attached to symbolic observances. We Christians, to whom so much of our native spiritual tradition is a closed book, have not altogether lost the sense of symbol. If it has not manifested itself in the liturgy, it is mainly because the liturgy has been so far closed to any cultural adaptation".[9]

During the two decades since these comments were made, liturgical experiments have been in varying degrees resisted, tolerated, permitted and encouraged. The millennial Hindu traditions of symbolism in worship would seem to render them all the more difficult of assimilation in Christian liturgy — at any rate in the eyes of a sizable segment of Indian Christians. Ultra-conservative groups apparently experience a morbid fear of Hinduisation of Christianity, whenever they see a tinge of the Hindu tradition in the ceremonials, statuary or iconography of Christian worship; they would eschew sedulously whatever even remotely suggests those 'pagan' links they have turned their backs upon.

The very concept of Religion may be at stake in such an attitude. One may justifiably wonder what Faith means to those who cling to cult in its imported garb, and refuse to perceive the import of cult in the expression of their Faith. The fact remains, however, that a Chosen-People mentality coupled with a self-righteous attitude has stalled inculturation in the sphere of worship. Some of the die-hards have gone so far as to constitute themselves into a 'Save-the-Faith' Movement in order to fight tooth and nail any intrusion of Hindu (or Indian?) element into the sanctuary. In some diseased minds Faith has become a damsel in distress to be rescued from the clutches of Hinduizers.

Fortunately, all is not lost. An appreciable number in the younger generation are discovering the need of integrating culture in the cult. The challenge of being the creators of a meaningful liturgy does appeal to them. As they progressively imbibe the mystery of God's covenant with Man, they will usher in the epiphany of God's Word in Man's idiom; they will at the same time favour a fruitful dialectic between the realities of life and their symbolic expression in worship. Thus the Word and Worship will be attuned to the evolving cultural milieux.

---

[9] Parmananda DIVARKAR, "Towards An Indian Liturgy", in *India And The Eucharist*, ed. by Lumen Institute, Ernakulam, India, 1964, p. 75.

3. A Humanity based on Justice

The tiny Christian communities of predominantly non-Christian countries face a great challenge: their faith has to be operative concurrently on two planes — one, in the task of knitting together those of the household in a visible communion of heart and mind; two, in the building up of a community-solidarity in the country as a whole, transcending the limited horizon of the Christian community. This would mean that the minority Christian community, impelled by the inner urge of authentic evangelization, makes a significant contribution in the evolving of Basic Communities of Peoples. These would be the realistic equivalent of the Basic Christian Communities of the Latin American countries which are in an analogous socio-political situation.

We take for our consideration three problem-areas in which the Christian communities could be actively assertive in the affirmation of their faith:

A. *The Caste-System*

Let us peer into the unique socio-cultural system which has engendered an iniquitous social stratification with no parallel in the world. 'Sanatana Dharma' or the Eternal Law is said to be the guide of the Caste-Model Society of India for the past 3000 years. In its worst manifestation it had produced a whole group of Untouchables. Mahatma Gandhi had christened them 'Harijans' or Children of God; he had declared untouchability a crime against God and Man. Today many Hindus would like to do away with the entire caste-system; yet modern electoral politics would only seem to polarise the different castes. What has been the message and what has been the action of Christian faith in such a situation?

The seed of Faith has been sown in the soil of a caste-ridden society by missionaries at different times with the fond hope that the Faith would eventually bring about a community based on the equality of the children of God. But unfortunately these hopes have been almost wholly belied. If anything, there has been a polarisation of caste within the Christian communities modelled on what is taking place in the larger Indian society.

Caste-divisiveness continues to be the bane of the Indian nation, which during these 38 years of independence has been tumbling along, aptly styled 'a functioning anarchy'. A strange type of morality of caste lays the axe at the root of a universal morality. "Only as members of family or caste do individuals become subjects of rights and obligations. Within these institutions the average Indian knows how to relate to others; outside them he is at a loss with neither norms nor guidelines to go by. That is why in the political sphere of bourgeois democracy which recognises the equality of all before the law the Indian behaves as though he is above the law. Equipped with the particularistic morality of caste, he is unable to cope with the universal morality of citizenship. Here lies the root of the crisis of morality in contemporary India".[10]

Has Faith helped the Christian communities to go beyond the morality of caste? Is there a sense of human equality within these communities? The anguished cry of Harijan Catholics gives a resounding NO for an answer. An open letter written in 1981 by some of these Catholics from Ramnad District in the State of Tamilnadu makes sad reading: "We are ashamed that we are discriminated against in Christianity which professes to be casteless. How is it that the Hierarchy does not seem to have made any attempt so far to speak in open terms during pastoral visits and in churches that casteism in Christianity is abominable? It is because we charish our faith and we love the Church that we take the liberty of expressing our sentiments. ... Even in our death we are not spared. Cemeteries are divided and one part is assigned for us with an impregnable wall dividing us from the so-called high-caste Catholics. It is to prevent our corpses walk past their area and contaminate it?"

Bold statement have not been wanting on the part of the Hierarchy. In January 1982 the C.B.C.I. (Catholic Bishops' Conference of India) held its plenary assembly at Tiruchirapalli and issued the following statement: "We state categorically that caste, with its consequent effects of discrimination and 'caste-mentality' has no place in Christianity. It is, in fact, a denial of Christianity because it is inhuman. It violates the God-given dignity and equality of the human person. ... It is an outright denial of the Fatherhood of God which, in practice, renders meaningless the brotherhood of man. ... The issue of caste and its consequent evil effects is not a

---

[10] Sebastian KAPPEN, *Jesus And Cultural Revolution,* op. cit., p. 63.

52

peripheral one for the Church or, indeed, for society at large. Delay in facing it — or sometimes even a refusal to do so — is more then a question of human rights. It is a betrayal of the Christian vocation".

Admirable words indeed: Within one kilometre of the venue of the Conference there is a Catholic cemetery in which 'low-caste' corpses are divided from the 'high-caste' ones by a wall of shame. Four years have passed since the C.B.C.I. declaration. The wall remains there. Inculturation of the Faith has not brought about any perceptible change to the Christian communities. Their cemeteries are as divided as those of non-Christians. Church authorities are reluctant to act upon their declarations. They want peace, peace at any cost — peace of the graveyard.

B. *Womanhood*

In the literacy campaigns for girls and in the sphere of higher education for women, Christian Churches have many things to their credit. There is some degree of emancipation for women in the Christian communities as compared with those of other religions in India. But in the area of marriage, more specifically in the functioning of the dowry-system most Christian communities tend to be replicas of the surrounding non-Christian cultures. Husbands are for sale, often for the highest bidder; brides and their families, in many cases, undergo untold hardships, even agonies before and after marriage. It is a slender consolation to note that bride-burning, a most shameful act of immolation of the married woman on the score that she has brought along insufficient dowry, reported in the papers now and then, is not heard of in Christian communities. Abolition of the dowry-system is a challenge Christian communities must face. Faith is yet to liberate them so that woman may receive full human dignity.

C. *Child-Labour*

It is a dismal world for children in India. For a century and more Christian missionaries have brought to millions of children in this land the blessing of education. Several organisations have followed suit. But given the population, the problem of child-care looks insoluble. We can count by the million the number of children who have never showed up at any school; and the drop-outs before the primary education is over will add up to a frightful figure.

The spirit of capitalism flourishes in a country which calls itself a Socialistic Democratic Republic. And illiterate children are an easy prey to avaricious entrepreneurs and contractors. In India capitalism operates in an economy of scarcity; child-labour is cheapest, and brings in ample returns of profit.

Christian communities, of themselves, cannot make a dent in this issue. But they can act as catalysts in the awakening of the larger community to the cruelties heaped upon children who are employed in thousands of cottage industries, and even in construction-works and mines. The Christian voice is not heard loud and clear. There are certain regions of child-labour in which Christian Churches are adequately present. Is it too much to expect that they lead or join groups with humanitarian motivations for the removal of the blot of child-labour from Indian culture?

PERSPECTIVES OF INCULTURATION IN INDIA

We may make a preliminary observation to say that all cultures carry with them three categories of elements: good, neutral, evil. Inculturation of the Faith in a particular context may be understood as the consolidation and enhancement of the good elements, and as the determined attempt at the eradication or at least the reduction of the evil elements bound with errors, superstitions and injustices: the motivation and the power to effect this should flow from the faith; and it should be the Christian community as such that undertakes this task. An attitude of neutrality had best be adopted towards the neutral elements in the local culture pertaining in general to food, clothing and social etiquette.

In the Indian situation Faith should bring a fresh glow to the lovable Indian traits of close family ties, hospitality and compassion, interiority and the quest for the Absolute. It should help eliminate or at least mitigate the forms of evil some of which we have mentioned above.

FAITH: LIBERATIVE and CREATIVE

The scope of Inculturation cannot be considered closed with the objectives mentioned above. A creative transformation of society should be the enduring objective of inculturation. Phrased differently, a continuing creation according to the design of the Creator should be the outcome of the flowering of the Faith implanted in human kind: man has to transcend man, for the Glory of God is Man fully Alive. This objective adds a futuristic component to the concept of inculturation, releasing it from the narrow restrictions foisted on its understanding.

An authentic inculturation in a Christian community should give rise to men and women who are themselves the Gospel-Creators of Tomorrow. For we deal ultimately with the power of Faith pulsating in the Heart of History. A resounding refusal to be the puppets of History is one of the main characteristics at once of Marxism and of Christianity. A cyclic view of human history — of emanation, re-absorption, re-emanation — belongs to religions which are a-historical. Judeo-Christian heritage carries with it a singular sense of history, not just a linear one, but one of a spiral nature with a thrust to the future.

FAITH: FOR A LIBERATION FROM BIRTH?

The predominant religious culture in India — the Hindu culture — postulates liberation from birth as the supreme attainment of the human beings. Christian faith tells us, on the other hand, that liberation from death is the divinely designed destiny for Man. Are we dealing here merely with a play on words or is there a stark contrast in the very substance of the different hopes nursed in the hearts of different religionists? 'Samsara' or the cycle of births is considered in the Hindu tradition as a fall from an original state of purity — of a pre-existing union with the Divine; a remerging with the Divine after a thorough purification in the course of several births is looked upon as Liberation from 'Samsara'.

The Christian Faith views the turmoil of the human condition in a totally different perspective. This is possibly summed up in the

55

cryptic passage of the 8th chapter of Paul's letter to the Romans: "The whole creation is eagerly awaiting for God to reveal his sons. ... From the beginning till now the entire creation, as we know, has been groaning in one great act of giving birth".

Liberation looked upon as release from the cycle of births has overtones of solitariness in the Hindu tradition. The liberation of being born as children of God after the 'groaning' has overtones of solidarity with the Liberator and with each other in the Christian tradition. This solidarity based on faith and hope commences in this life and is to be consummated in the next.

LIBERATION FROM SUFFERING: VIEWPOINTS

Intimately linked with the doctrine of 'Samsara' is the theory of the transmigration of souls. 'Karma', as it is popularly spelt out in religious parlance, would imply that all evil is the outcome of sins committed in the past. These have to be expiated by the individuals who committed them, if need be, through a succession of lives. There is no question of vicarious suffering as in Christianity. One who may come to the relief of another cannot effectively take away his suffering; by his good action he accumulates merit for himself, but only helps postpone the suffering of the other without being able to delete it altogether. It is against this religious backdrop that we must assess the apathy of the average Hindu towards the suffering of his neighbour. His compassion may indeed prove to be effective on occasion, but he is not convinced he is blotting out the 'karma' of the other.

The attitude to suffering in the Christian communities of India may very well be a mixture of three strands: one, a questionable brand of resignation akin to the fatalism of 'karma'; two, a laudable acceptance of it in view of a greater conformity with the suffering Christ; three, a longing for deliverance from it, the longing being grounded in the Hope of liberation even here and now through the salvific suffering of the Saviour. It is easy to understand there is a resignation close passivity, stemming from the larger religious climate in which one moves. Passivity in the face of suffering and union with the Passion of Christ are worlds apart from each other. They may possibly alternate in the same person. The devotion of suffering Christians to the Passion of Our Lord is a touching manifestation of their love for Him. Most edifying is the spectacle of congregations following the Stations of the Cross on the Lenten Fridays of sizzling summers. Certain visible signs of union with the Suffering Servant are a remarkable phenomenon of the Christian community.

It is in the longing for liberation from suffering that we have to perceive the role of inculturation. What posture does the Christian community adopt vis-à-vis the vast man-made suffering which is their lot? Their burden is often enough some form of oppression imposed on them by their fellow human beings. Those who long for deliverance from the oppression might pray fervently, and yet do nothing to bring about their own liberation. Or this liberation might be sought as a ripe fruit expected to drop right into the hollow of their hands, whereas it should normally be the outcome of their own human efforts. Indeed these efforts are an important part of the social process for which, however, they have not been prepared by their spiritual and social psychology. A genuine inculturation would indicate the link between Faith and the struggle for justice.

The Marginalised on the March

All the young Churches, barring the notable exception of the Japanese Church, belong to the Third World. Referring to Bandung, the first explosion of protest against oppression and the emergence of the Third World as a group of nations, Marie-Dominique Chenu observes: "This Third World is emerging onto the social, political and religious stage of world history. This is an extraordinary mutation charged with hopes and anguish. ... Our own business here is to take the measure of the dimensions of the mutation in the theology that is secretly at the heart of all the other mutations — to seize what are its living insights, its contexts, its methods, its scope. Shall we not be seeing a new theology — in the way that Latin theology was new in relation to eastern theology? ... My perception is that those who refuse this theology are just those who paid no attention to the famous Bandung Conference in 1955 ... enclosed in their supernaturalism which fails to see the singleness

57

of man's vocation and which thereby disjoins liberation from eschatological salvation".[11]

A question most relevant to the marginalised peoples of India would be this: do her Christian communities project a vision of liberation from evil both in the present life and in the next? With their moorings in Jewish history, the Christian communities ought to raise their eyes to God, not so much as to One Who is there just to be adored, as to One Who is their Liberator. The Old and the New Testaments provide paradigms of liberation rooted in the faith of a Saviour-God, because He is one who listens to the cry of His people. Every Christian who is true to his calling realises his responsibility towards his people far beyond the boundaries of personal moral uprightness. "The Christian is not just the person who has clean hands. Resistance is a legitimate part of Christian life and Christian ethics. And we have no reason to be ashamed of it. Resistance is also a responsibility".[12] Resistance, especially to the burden placed on the people on the march, is a sharing of the burden the Saviour has assumed.

A HORIZON THAT IS BECKONING

An invocation of the hoary past may urge us to reach out to the unreachable star. The millennial prayer of India couched in the lovely verse of the Brihadaranyaka Upanishad echoes poignantly in millions of hearts to day:

> From the Unreal, Lead me to the Real
> From Darkness, lead me to the Light
> From Death, lead me to Immortality

Darkness and Death may indeed be today the daily portion of the marginalised brothers and sisters of our land. A tiny minority leads

---

[11] Maria-Dominique Chenu, "A New Birth: Theologians of the Third World", in Elizondo/Greinacher (Ed.), *Tensions Between The Churches Of The First World And The Third World* (CONCILIUM 144) pp. 18, 20.

[12] Orthodox Bishop Mar Paulose of India, quoted by Victor P. KARUNAN, "An Asian Example", in *People's Movements And Christian Discernment*, Pro Mundi Vita, Bulletin 98, 1984/3, p. 23.

an unreal life in arrogant opulence, and institutional violence holds sway. In this sinister scene Jesus the Truth, the Light and the Life is beckoning to the Church to take the plunge.

It would not be realistic to expect from the Indian Churches a totally unified perception of India today: the picture is frightfully bewildering. However, inspired by the same Faith and desirous of serving the same Lord, they may not find it impossible to approach the problems in their milieux with attitudes and policies similar in their broad contours. In the first place the Church leaders, both clerical and lay, will have to shed an imaginary harmonic model of society. That India is a land of 'ahimsa' (non-violence) is largely a myth. There is violence, latent and eruptive, at every level of society. Irenism or Peace-at-any-cost is not going to remedy the situation. An understanding of Faith, active and revolutionary, is essential if the Christian communities mean to help the country march to liberation. When authentic human values of truth and service, love and compassion are being thrown to the winds, a cultural revolution constantly engendered by the Faith may well be the enduring response inculturation offers to the human situation. In a context soaked in social sin Faith ought to be a subversive force, precisely because it is a re-creative force.

THE CALL FOR AN INCULTURATED APOSTOLATE

With an enlightened understanding of a revolutionary faith the Indian Churches should undertake an evaluation, and where and in the measure needed, a re-vamping of their apostolate. Education, Health and Social Service have been the important sectors, traditionally, of the Church apostolate in India. We shall touch upon the significance of inculturation in the two areas of education and social service.

The apostolate of education is a long-standing and con-ventional one in the Indian Churches. A sizable portion of their personnel and resources have been invested in it. On the one hand, this apostolate has served the poor, especially among the Christians, in different parts of India. On the other, with an eye for their survival, the Churches have tended to serve the oppressor-classes in the higher reaches of education, and have thus stabilised the capitalistic system; the minority-complex of the Churches has been manifest in such a service. By the same token the value-system operative in such a service has been one aligned with that of the powerful minority in the country. This has especially been true where English has been adopted as the medium of instruction. It is true that English-medium schools are sought after both by the rich and the poor, though only the rich can survive in them long enough to profit by them. Many Christian missionaries linked with them have earned the image of the servants of the rich, and the purveyors of an alien culture.

An evaluation of the investment in the educational apostolate is an urgent need today. It has been claimed that English-medium schools and the institutions serving the privileged few are points of insertion in the local non-Christian community. It is a claim difficult to accept. Sociologically the entry-points for any Christian missionary should be the life-struggle of the people whom he/she wants to evangelize. A grass-roots worker thus outlines the task before us: "As Christians we are challenged to identify and integrate with the socio-cultural, religious, ethnic specificity of our societies. This identity alone will provide us with the necessary rapport in order to gain the confidence of the poor and work together with them for change in society. ... Christians today are challenged to intervene historically in the situation and reality of our people. This reality alone will help us to evaluate the relevance or irrelevance of our Christian presence in society".[13]

Feeble stirrings are perceived today in many of our educational institutions which begin to profess that they would like to turn their students into agents of social change. If indeed they adopt effective programmes for the implementation of their new-found ideal, they may have to pay a high price. In the early centuries of the Christian era martyrs for the faith sacrificed their lives in the cause of upholding true doctrine concerning Jesus and His Church. Bearing witness to Jesus today often means fighting for justice to be done to His least brethren. If our educational institutions take up this cause, as they should, they may face harassment of all sorts, and even the danger of extinction. If inculturation leads them upto that destiny, their very death will be

---

[13] Victor P. KARUNAN, op. cit., p. 27.

most fruitful in generating individuals and groups determined to bring about a more humane and just society.

We are now led to weigh the significance of the social services of the Churches as an expression of their Faith. Social Service is a generic term which includes social work and social action. An impressive number of the personnel of the Churches have been active in social work; purely charitable services of mercy and compassion have brought relief to thousands upon thousands of the poor. In most cases they have not been an unmixed blessing, as they have tended to create an attitude of dependence in the beneficiaries. During the past three decades another form of social work has taken shape: multi-purpose service societies have sprung up in many dioceses in view of development work and of adult education; the societies are mostly dependent on funding agencies abroad. There is no denying that the services rendered by these societies are a step forward in the promotion of the human person. Yet one will hesitate to consider them as an expression of the inculturation of the Faith in a Christian community. For the community itself is largely a recipient of the services.

It is in social action that a Christian community can give ample evidence of the fecundity of the Faith it bears. Gone are the days when charities and relief services could be looked upon as the panacea for societal ills. Human societies all over the world have acquired a mass of information, and subsequently scientific knowledge regarding their own functioning regionally, nationally and in the international sphere. An enlightened faith necessarily profits by this knowledge. Hence during the past three decades or so, in Christian circles, Faith-and Justice has tended to replace Faith-and-Charities as the target for the human race. In India, given the magnitude of human destitution, the Churches have continued to lay a heavy accent on charities as the expression of their faith. But a serious awakening is taking place among the enlightened laity, clergy and religious. A recent controversy, dating from the early 80s and aired in the Press illustrates the pulls and tensions within the Christian communities regarding the participation of priests and religious in the fight for justice. One Sister Alice who undertook a long fast supporting the agitation of poor fisherfolk for their rights became a symbol of the Church fighting for justice. Mother Teresa of international fame continued to be the symbol of the Indian Church of love and compassion. Alice or Teresa? This was the question bandied about for some time. Whom does India need? A felicitous response was not long in coming: India needs more and more of Alices, and less and less of Teresas. The episcopal censure of the part played by priests and religious in communion with the fisherfolk fighting for justice only served to reveal the reactionary stance of some Bishops; these would want the Church to help the victims of injustice, and not attempt to eradicate the causes of injustice — or at any rate would like to keep the clergy and the religious away from the struggle of the common man. It is a healthy sign of the inculturation of the faith in the Christian community as a whole that more and more persons drawn from the laity, the clergy and the religious life find themselves at the crossroads of social conflict, taking the side of the marginalised.

The crucial challenges of inculturation in the Indian situation can be succinctly summed up: the local communities of Christians are called upon to give a faith-response to the twin-aspiration of their countrymen — the liberation of Man in the contemplation of the Absolute. The response should show the Way to Freedom from the Bondage of Sin and all its consequences; and the response should flow from a deep communion with the Word and from a deeply meaningful Worship which blends with the Indian cultures.

A TAILPIECE

Inculturating young Churches the world over have a positive contribution to offer to the Universalism of Christianity. The triumphs and tragedies spanning the twenty centuries of the Christian era are leading mankind to the discovery of new values of global dimensions. The East-West confrontation in culture, philosophy and religion is yielding to the North-South Dialogue apparently of a more materialist nature; yet largely on the outcome of this dialogue will depend the well-being of mankind as a whole. The contribution of the young Churches can make a qualitative difference to the resolution of the Dialogue.

St Joseph's College
Tiruchirapalli 620 002 — India

ARUL M. VARAPRASADAM, S.J.

Kees Bertens, MSC

THE CATHOLIC COMMUNITY IN INDONESIA
AND THE PROBLEM OF INCULTURATION

1. A historical note

In 1984 the Catholic Church of Indonesia celebrated the four hundred and fiftieth anniversary of her existence. The celebration took place at the level of the parishes, the dioceses and finally at the national level during a five-day meeting in July in the capital city of Jakarta that involved the participation of the whole Indonesian Episcopate and delegates of all the dioceses. The expected presence of Pope John Paul II did not materialize, but nevertheless the celebration was a very happy and encouraging event in the life of this Asian branch of the Catholic Church. In fact there is historical evidence that there were Indonesian Christians much earlier than 1534. The Egyptian historian Abu Salih al-Armini informs us that there were already Christians about the middle of the seventh century in West Sumatra, in the present diocese of Sibolga;[1] and in the thirteenth and fourteenth centuries Franciscan missionaries visited the Indonesian islands and baptized people there. However, the Christian communities of these times did not survive in history, and it was only in the sixteenth century that Portuguese missionaries started to evangelize systematically in the Moluccas. The year 1534 is considered as the beginning of the Catholic Church in Indonesia, when the local prince of Moro, in the north of the island Halmahera, was baptized together with many of his subjects.[2] Since that date Indonesia has always had a Catholic community although not until the end of the nineteenth and the beginning of the twentieth century was evangelization carried out very intensively. The establishment of the Catholic Hierarchy by Pope John XXIII on 3 January 1961 may be considered as the crowning of many years of mission labour.

---

[1] Y. BAKKER SJ, in: *Sejarah Gereja Katolik Indonesia,* Vol. I, Ende-Flores, 1974, p. 27-36.

[2] B. VISSER MSC, *Onder Spaansch-Portugeesche vlag,* Amsterdam, 1925, p. 7-11.

2. *The land and the people*

Indonesia is the largest archipelago in the world. The outer limits of this 6000 km stretch of islands is as far as California is from Bermuda or as far as the west coast of Ireland is from the Caspian Sea. Its sea area is four times larger than its land area. Indonesians call their country "Tanah Air Kita" ("Our Land and Water"). Of the more than 13,000 islands that make up its territory only 992 have permanent inhabitants. But most of the 155 million Indonesians live on the five big islands of Java, Sumatra, Kalimantan, Sulawesi and Irian Jaya (the last is the former Dutch New Guinea), which cover more than 90% of the total territory. In this extensive archipelago live many ethnic groups, each with their own language, traditions and culture. There are more than 250 different languages. It may be considered a unique achievement that all these different ethnic groups have been united through the use of one national language, "bahasa Indonesia", a modernized version of the Malay language. Everywhere except in a few remote areas, one can communicate with the local people in this common language. Radio and television play an important role in creating this situation. One can see why the Indonesian government has given the highest priority to the expensive communication satellite project called "Palapa". The biggest and most influential ethnic group are the Javanese, who live in Central and East Java and — in ever growing numbers — in transmigration areas outside Java. There are about 70 million Javanese, i.e. 45% of the total Indonesian population.

When we realize this geographical and cultural situation, we can easily understand why the Republic of Indonesia has as its national motto: "Bhinneka Tunggal Ika" (unity in diversity).[3] A more appropriate motto is hard to imagine. And when we view the young nation's political history, in my opinion, the conclusion is justified that this motto has not remained a mere ideal, although sometimes the national unity has been tested dramatically.

Also in the religious field Indonesia displays a great diversity. According to the government census of 1980 the breakdown of the

---

[3] This is not Indonesian, but Sanskrit, a language that in Indonesia plays a role similar to that of Latin in European coats of arms.

population by religion is as follows: 87.19% Moslem, 5.77% Protestant, 2.96% Catholic, 2.03% Hindu, 0.92% Buddhist, 1.10 other religions. Although the majority of Indonesians are Moslems, Indonesia is not an Islamic state. In 1945 Sukarno, one of the founding fathers and the first president, resolutely defeated efforts in that direction by formulating the "Pancasila" (the five principles) as the foundation of the new state. The first principle is faith in one God. The proposal to add that the Islamic Law would be obligatory for all its faithful was dropped, in order to meet the objections of the Christians. "Pancasila" still remains a decisive factor in the unity of the young state and has been considerably corroborated during the "new order" of President Suharto.

3. *From the Church's statistics*

In 1940 there were 566,302 Catholics; in 1960, 1,302,732; in 1980, 4,355,575. Of the last number 32% live in Flores (the only island that has an almost completely Catholic population) and 18% in Java. Of the 570 priests there were in 1940, only 3% were Indonesian; of the 1,069 priests in 1960, 14% were Indonesian; and of the 1,667 priests in 1980, 46% were Indonesian. Of the 520 brothers there were in 1940, 9% were Indonesian; of the 600 in 1960, 24% were Indonesian; and of the 758 in 1980, 69% were Indonesian. The increase was fastest among the sisters: of the 1,841 sisters in 1940, only 9% were Indonesian; of the 2,573 in 1960, 35% were Indonesian; and of the 4,306 in 1980, 82% were Indonesian.

The Catholic Church in Indonesia is divided into 33 dioceses (excluding the diocese Dili of East Timor). When Pope Paul VI visited Indonesia in 1970, there were no bishops to welcome him at the airport. The bishops were gathered in the cathedral, where the Pontiff went immediately after his arrival and address the men and women religious. This was arranged on purpose, so that not too much attention from the national and international press would be attracted to the fact that the majority of the bishops were still foreigners (or Indonesian naturalized foreigners). At that moment, of the 33 bishops and apostolic prefects there were only 5 native Indonesians. In January 1986 the 33 dioceses were led by 22 native Indonesian bishops and 10 foreign bishops or apostolic administrators, while one bishop's see was vacant. In the future it is not likely that another foreign missionary will be appointed bishop: there are enough Indonesian candidates.

4. *Inculturation*

"Inculturation" is a key word in theological reflection in Indonesia. "Inculturation" — or "Indonesianization", as is heard more often here —, has been and still is a regular topic on the agenda of the annual meeting of the Indonesian Bishops' Conference. It was a main issue for the national congress on liturgy a few years ago. And it has already been the general theme for a national meeting of the Indonesian Association of Religious Men and Women. More often yet has it been and will it be in the future the theme for informal discussion on all levels of Church life.

Let me begin with what I would like to call the material side of the inculturation of the Indonesian Church. The Indonesian Catholic Church is becoming more and more independent of outside assistance, especially insofar as personnel is concerned. (Independence in the financial sector is less stressed.) The role of the foreign missionary is no longer vital for the survival of the local Church, and appearance amidst the Catholic community is becoming relativeluy rare. Nearly all the leading functions in the Church have passed or will in the near future pass into Indonesian hands. Particularly in the congregations of Sisters (with their relatively short period of formation) development took a fast course. However, we should immediately add that the situation is not the same in all parts of Indonesia. There are, for instance, dioceses that have hardly any clergy of their own. Especially in the dioceses of the province of Irian Jaya the situation is very difficult. Nevertheless this material side of Indonesianization confronts many missionaries with the often painful question of whether they would do better to retire and look for a field of activity elsewhere.

But more important yet is the formal side of inculturation. I should like to try to compare the briefly sketched situation in the Indonesian Church with the description of the process of inculturation given by Father A. Roest Crollius. He writes: "the inculturation of the Church is the integration of the Christian experience of a local Church into the culture of its people, in such a way that this experience not only expresses itself in elements of this culture, but becomes a force that animates, orients and innovates this culture so as to create a new unity and communion, not only within the culture in question but also as an enrichment of the Church universal".[4]

When we restrict ourselves to the first part of this description or, as the same author puts it, when we consider inculturation as "the process by which the Church becomes invested in a given culture",[5] then we can see that the insertion of the Catholic Church (and the Christian Churches in general) did succeed quite well. The Christian Churches are not a *corpus alienum* in Indonesian society. As we have seen before, the situation of the Christians in Indonesia is that of a small minority amidst a large majority of Moslems; but, although all sectors of Indonesian society are coloured by this widespread Moslem presence, Indonesia is not an Islamic nation. The national ideology, the "Pancasila", is acknowledged and received by all religions. Moreover, the Indonesian Constitution of 1945 guarantees freedom of religion. Christians in Indonesia do not live in the ghetto conditions that can be observed in some other Asian countries. Protestants and Catholics can be found in all areas of social, political, and cultural life. The present Chief of Staff of the Indonesian Army is a Catholic and there have been several Protestant ones before. Almost each cabinet in Indonesian history has included a number of Christian ministers and there are Christian officials on all levels of the army, the government and the diplomatic service. Christians participate whole-heartedly in the national development programs that have been started since President Suharto took office in the mid-sixties. The decisive reason for this full participation of Christians in national life is that from the start they took part in the nation's struggle for independence. This independence struggle was a nationalistic movement, open to Indonesians of all religious convictions. Since Catholics and Protestants unhesitatingly participated fully in that movement, it was clear to everyone that a Christian can be a good patriot too.

---

[4] A. ROEST CROLLIUS SJ, *What is so new about inculturation?*, Rome, Pontifical Gregorian University, p. 15-16.
[5] *Ibid.*, p. 6.

After the transfer of sovereignty by the Dutch on 27 December 1949 the Christians supported the claim of the Indonesian government that Dutch New Guinea should be an integral part of Indonesian territory. In this longlasting affair (it was not settled until 1963) it once again became clear that the Christian Churches in Indonesia could not be identified with their origin in the colonial period.

In a voluminous book the Dutch missiologist M. Muskens has analysed the situation of the Catholic Church in Indonesia against the background of the struggle between Moslems and nationalists in their mutual search for national identity. The author has also travelled extensively through Pakistan, India and Thailand and visited all the Catholic centers there. His main question was: "Why is it that the Catholic Church in Indonesia, unlike in the other three countries, has been so well integrated? ... In Pakistan, India and Thailand the Catholics live outside the cultural traditions of these countries, which traditions are completely dominated by Islam, Hinduism and Buddhism respectively".[6] His answer is that in Indonesia it was not a certain religious group (Islam) but the nationalists under the leadership of Sukarno that prevailed in the formation of a national identity. In this respect they could make use of the integrating tendency that characterizes Indonesians — and Javanese in particular.

5. A problematic culture

Why do we speak of the inculturation of the Catholic community in Indonesia as a problem? Because Indonesian culture itself is problematic. It is not very clear what should be understood by "Indonesian culture", because the country is fundamentally pluricultural. When people in Indonesia speak about "culture", what is usually understood is one of the traditional local cultures: the culture of the Javanese, the Sundanese, the Balinese, the Bataks or the many other peoples of the archipelago. The mass media often present elements of these local cultures: dances, Wayang performances,[7]

---

[6] M. MUSKENS, *Indonesië. Een strijd om nationale identiteit* (with a summary in English), Bussum, 1970, p. 481.

[7] "Wayang" is the dramatic puppet theatre of Java and Bali, based on ancient epics that originate from India.

instrumental music, songs, architecture, traditional costumes, paintings and carvings. Among these local cultures the biggest and most influential is the Javanese culture (together with the related Balinese culture), although, for non-Javanese, Javanese culture remains to a great extent an alien element, and it is yet more obvious that the Javanese remains an outsider with respect to the cultures of the other islands. In the Catholic Church many of those cultural elements are integrated: there are several churches built in the style of the local architecture; there are church songs that make use of native melodies; [8] especially in the liturgy such elements are used. So inculturation in this sense is often connected with some specific local Indonesian culture.

But apart from these cultures we are also witnesses to a modern Indonesian culture that is still in the making. We see for instance that artists elaborate elements of a traditional local culture into modern forms. For Indonesian Christians inculturation does not only mean adjustment to an already existing culture, because Indonesian culture itself is still in flux. For them inculturation also means participation in the creation of that new Indonesian culture. The single unifying Indonesian language, which is still in development, is, in my opinion, a very important part of the modern Indonesian culture that is in formation now. In this context, it could be observed that Christians pray in their own national language, whereas the Moslems pray in Arabic. Among Catholics, the renewal of the liturgy after the second Vatican Council passed off without any problems. Although at first there could be heard voices that pointed out the necessity of a sacral language in worship (such as the Arabic of the Moslems), I do not know of any religious services in Latin in Indonesia.

6. *The deeper dimension of inculturation*

Now I have to try to answer the question of whether the second part of Fr. Roest Crollius' description of inculturation can also be

---

[8] Since two years ago there has been interesting attempt to introduce a song-book that collects several local melodies together with European and Gregorian melodies.

applied to the Catholic community in Indonesia. Can we say that the Christian experience of the Catholic community in Indonesia is taking place "in such a way that this experience not only expresses itself in elements of this culture, but becomes a force that animates, orients and innovates this culture so as to create a new unity and communion, not only within the culture in question but also as an enrichment of the Church universal"? The question is not an easy one, but I would nevertheless like to attempt an answer via a detour.

The well-known French theologian Yves Congar in several of his publications distinguishes four fundamental functions of the Church. These four functions are: (a) to bear witness to the gospel of salvation in Jesus Christ (*martyria*); (b) celebration of this salvation in the liturgy (*leitourgia*); (c) the living of a communal brotherhood (*koinonia*); (d) service to others (*diakonia*).[9] The above-mentioned question may be to some extent answered when we try to look at the situation of the Indonesian Church in connection with these four elements.

(a) It could be said that the testimony of Indonesian Catholics is not too bad, when we consider the constant increase of the Church. For example, in 1984 the Archdiocese of Jakarta had 7,647 adult catechumens[10] of a total number of 220,588 faithful. The Churches obviously exercise attractive power. It is not of course always possible to discover the motivation of these people, which will usually be very complex. But I was personally informed a couple of times that people felt attracted to the Church by the way Catholics lived. Apart from this, in Indonesia one must be very careful with evangelization, particularly since in 1978 the Ministry of Religious Affairs forbade the propagation of a religion among people who already adhere to another religion.

(b) When inculturation is discussed, liturgy is often given special or even almost exclusive attention. I mentioned earlier that in Indonesia elements of the local cultures are received in the

---

[9] E.g. in *Eglise catholique et France moderne*, Paris, Hachette, 1978. In a short note on inculturation a young Indonesian theologian, J. BANAWIRATNA SJ, has pointed out that inculturation should be given shape in these four functions of the Church: "Inkulturasi", *Rohani*, 1982, p. 361-366.

[10] Pupils of elementary and secondary schools are included here.

liturgy. In this respect Catholics are often more willing than Protestants. The latter show more reservations, because they are suspicious of the pagan background of the native cultures. Nevertheless, even in the Catholic churches this use of autochton elements in the liturgy tends to be an exception. A church visitor from outside gets the general impression of a rather traditional (in the European sense) shape of the liturgy.

(c) The living of a communal brotherhood has its paradigmal expression in the young Church (Acts 2,41-47). Can we find something in the Catholic Church in Indonesia that recalls this primordial Christian community? Perhaps we can. The sense of community is very strong in Indonesia, and this applies to Catholics too. Catholics know each other and it is soon found out if a newcomer is a Catholic. The mission stations in the countryside are often living communities (mostly without a permanent priest). But the same can been seen in the cities. The parishes in the cities, that often cover a large area, are usually divided into districts, which in their turn are divided into "circles" (*lingkungan*) or whatever the name that is used. The functioning may not be expected to be always ideal. Tensions or even conflicts can happen, usually about very trivial affairs. But also in the young Church there were already conflicts. Nevertheless these circles are often truly living communities of Christian faith and form the very core of parish life. Such a circle will consist of about 30 families who regularly meet to pray (for example the rosary in May), to read Holy Scripture or to celebrate the Eucharist. There is a leader and, in keeping with the Indonesian feeling for heavy organizational structures, there are several officials. But the advantage is that it involves many people. Newcomers are visited and invited to participate in the activities. When a member becomes unemployed jobs are looked for. When somebody is seriously ill or dies, the whole circle is ready to give its help and sympathy. The functioning of a circle to a large extend depends on the leader — who is not seldom a woman. And in the meetings poor and well-to-do faithful can be found together in true brotherhood. Although the term is not used, a circle like that is often what elsewhere would be named a "basic community".

(d) As already mentioned, "mutual service" often takes place spontaneously in the circles. Apart from this, a parish usually possesses a committee for social assistance. For many years now there has been a yearly Lent-action in imitation of the Catholic Church in the countries of Western Europe. But this cannot be considered a mere imitation of Western ideas. It constitutes an element of genuine inculturation, because also the Moslems have their obligation of alms for the poor (*zakat*) at the end of their Ramadan fast-period. The yearly collection for the Catholic orphanages of Jakarta is always a great success. In the case of a national disaster or a difficult political situation such as in East Timor the Catholic community will certainly respond. And would it be far-fetched to see mutual service also in the fact that Catholics are often known for their honesty? In a country where corruption rages at all levels, a Catholic is often looked for as a treasurer, because people have confidence in his honesty.

* * *

These short notes may suffice to show that as far as the Catholic Church of Indonesia is concerned there are reasons to answer the above-mentioned question positively. It is certainly very difficult and perhaps even impossible to measure this deeper dimension of inculturation efficaciously. Inculturation in this sense will more often remain an ideal than a concrete reality.

7. *Some perspectives*

I would like to conclude these reflections with an attempt to formulate some personal observations and experiences that give way to some perspectives that may be interesting for other young Churches as well.

— Comparisons between East and West are often over-simplified, whereas the reality is far more complicated. For me this was never clearer than in the following experience. Tomohon is a small town in the mountains of the province of North Sulawesi. It is the center of the local Protestant Church, the seat of the synod, with a faculty of theology for the training of ministers, a hospital and several types of schools. There are also two Catholic parishes, a number of Catholic schools directed by Sisters and Brothers, and a Catholic hospital. Both on the Protestant and the Catholic side there are several foreign missionaries from the U.S.A., Holland and Switzerland. For some years there was also a Japanese doctor who worked for the Protestant hospital. The local Indonesians thought that the Japanese and his wife were rather strange with their odd curtseys and gestures, whereas they had no difficulty at all with the manners of the Americans and Europeans present there. Once an Indonesian happened to collect a daughter of the Japanese at the near-by airport and bring her to the house of her parents. He was extremely surprised, witnessing the Japanese welcome home which was so strange to him: Eastern manners were for the Oriental stranger that Western ones!

— The devotional strain in the Catholic community of Indonesia is very strong. Candles, images, novenas and pilgrimages are very popular; this is also go among the newly baptized. Obviously these expressions of popular religion are strongly anchored in the religious soul and are not exclusively Western. On the other hand it must be added that this devotional interest is less exuberant in Indonesia than in countries evangelized by southern European missionaries such as the neighbouring country of the Philippines.

— A local church that has reached a certain level of inculturation (a process never completely finished) should become a missionary force in the Church. Inculturation must never annul catholicity. In Indonesia some congregations of Priests, Brothers and Sisters have already started mission activities on a modest scale. They have sent missionaries to difficult areas in their own country (such as Irian Jaya and Kalimantan) and even abroad (Africa, Papua New Guinea, the Fiji Islands). Government regulations greatly hamper the acquisition of visas; otherwise there would certainly be more exchanges of Indonesian missionaries with foreign ones (for instance Filipinos).

— In the capital of a developing country such as Indonesia there are many foreigners: diplomats, employees of banks and other firms, experts sent by their respective government, etc. There are regularly religious services for the Catholics among them I do not possess any exact figures on the total situation, but I see and hear that services for the Dutch, Germans and French are poorly attended, whereas services for South Koreans are very well attended. A few years ago there happened to be a rather big group of Japanese Catholics who were notably ardent. When we consider also the full churches we can witness in Indonesia, I wonder if the predictions of Father Bühlmann are not coming to fulfilment before our eyes, when he says that the centre of the Church is moving outside Europe and Northern America.[11] And will then the problem of inculturation not become a problem of transculturation?

KEES BERTENS, MSC

---

[11] Walbert BÜHLMANN OFM Cap., *The coming of the Third Church*, Slough (England), St. Paul Publications, 1976.

J.B. Banawiratma, S.J.

A PNEUMATOLOGICAL APPROACH
TO INCULTURATION

Why do we take this approach? The experience of the Holy Spirit is precisely our experience of faith. "No one can say 'Jesus is the Lord' except by the Holy Spirit" (1 Cor 12:3). And when "we cry 'Abba! Father!' it is the Spirit himself bearing witness with our spirit that we are children of God" (Rom 8:15f).

A pneumatological approach to inculturation is an approach through the Church's experience of the Holy Spirit. It is an approach based on our faith in the Spirit of God who is living and working in the Church, in the world's cultures. Since it is an approach through the experiences of the Church, first we will see at least some experiences which indicate the process of inculturation.

1. *Some Indications of Conscious Efforts towards Inculturation in Indonesia*

The first experience of people *hearing the Gospel* and believing in Jesus Christ the Son of God is an experience of a *community* of Christians. The Christian people try to live and to act as Christians. In Java, for example, the people ask whether it is allowed or not to make a traditional, communal feast called *"slametan"*.[1] Such an experience is similar to the one the Corinthian people had: May a Christian eat food consecrated to a pagan god? (cfr. 1 Cor 8:1-13).

The next step of their experience is a conscious effort to deepen their religious life. They build groups of basic communities locally of functionally. Their communal experience expresses itself in a form of ecclesiastical organisation at the level of parish, like functional groups of parish, parish council, etc.

---

[1] *Slamet* means peaceful: nothing disturbs one's life. "At the center of the whole Javanese religious system lies a simple, formal, undramatic, almost furtive, little ritual: the *slametan* (also sometimes called a *kenḍu – ren*). The *slametan* is the Javanese version of what is perhaps *the world's most common religious ritual, the communal feast, and, as almost everywhere, it symbolizes the mystic and social unity of those participating in it*. Friends, neighbors, fellow workers, relatives, local

The people in the basic communities try to help each other in understanding the Gospel. They read the Scriptures, they give witness to one another about their faith in Jesus Christ. The second National Congress of Catechesis (June 28 - July 5, 1980) [2] talked about the "community-catechesis" ("Katekese umat"). *Community-catechesis* is understood as communication of faith or sharing of faith among the members of the community. Through their witness to each other they strengthen their faith. In the "community-catechesis" the stress lies upon the experience ("penghayatan"), although the importance of knowledge is not forgotten or put aside. The community-catechesis is a catechesis of the people by the people. The function of the leader is to create an atmosphere conducive to communication; the leader guides the communication. The congress formulates the goal of the community-catechesis as follows:

— seeing daily experiences in the light of the Gospel;
— conversion (*metanoia*) to God and becoming more conscious of the presence of God in the daily realities;

---

spirits, dead ancestors, and nearforgotten gods all get bound, by virtue of their commensality, into a defined social group pledged to mutual support and cooperation. In Modjokuto the *slametan forms a kind of social universal joint, fitting the various aspects of social life and individual experience together in a way which minimizes uncertainty, tension, and conflict* — or at least it is supposed to do so. The altered form of twentieth-century urban and suburban life in Java makes it rather less efficient as an integrating mechanism and rather less satisfying as a religious experience for many people; but among the group here described as *abangan* — the more traditionalized peasants and their proletarianized comrades in the towns — the *slametan* still retains much of its original force and attraction.

A *slametan* can be given in reponse to almost any occurrence one wishes to celebrate, ametiorate, or sanctify. Birth, marriage, sorcery, death, house moving, bad dreams, harvest, name-changing, opening a factory, illness, supplication of the village guardian spirit, circumcision, and starting off a political meeting may all occasion a *slametan*. For each the emphasis is slightly different. One part or another of the total ritual is intensified and elaborated; another part is toned down. The mood changes somewhat, but the underlying structure of the ritual remains the same. There is always the special food (differing according to the intent of the *slametan*); there is always incense, the Islamic chant, and the extra-formal high-Javanese speech of the host (its content, too, naturally, varying with the occasion); and there is always the polite, embarrassed, muted manner which suggests that, despite the brevity and lack of drama the ritual displays, *something important is going on*." (C. Geertz, *The Religion of Java*, N.Y., 1960, 11-12).

[2] Th. HUBER, *Katekese umat, Hasil pertemuan kateketik antar keuskupan se Indonesia II*, Yogyakarta 1981 (Kanisius).

80

— growth, consequently, in faith, hope and love and strengthening of our christian life;

— greater unity in Christ, and growth as people of God able to carry out the mission of the local Church so as to strengthen the universal Church;

— willingness to give witness to Christ through our life in society.

Another faith-experience of the Christian people is the *liturgical celebration*. Here the Christian Community prays in the name of Jesus the Lord. Three years ago (1980) the Indonesian Bishops' Commission for Liturgy published a book of prayers and songs *Madah Bakti*. As a conscious effort to realize inculturation in the field of liturgy *Madah Bakti* pays much attention to regional songs. The third National Congress of Liturgy (July 8-13, 1980) [3] had "Inculturation of Liturgy" as its central theme. This theme supports the Church's concern for expressing and realizing christian faith authentically.

Speaking about experience and authentic expression of faith we note the contributions of *Indonesian art* as, for example, in painting and architecture. A group of artists from Bali paints stories and events of the Scripture in Balinese style. Ir. Mangunwijaya pr. tried to build several churches in Central Java based on people's experience of the Javanese house. [4] We don't want here to enter into the complexity of Javanese housing with its agricultural background. It is enough to note two ideas. First, there is the idea of "open area", a place where the communication of the living Church happens. This idea is connected with experience of God which is linked with the experience of nature, heaven and earth, an experience of openness before God in this pilgrimage of life (cf. the experience of Israel in the desert). The second is the symbol of the "womb" (Indonesian: *rahim* means also merciful). The womb gives birth to a new person. In the symbol of the womb we find also the dialectic between "outside" and "inside", "light" and "dark". We are called to come to the mystery of the divine life as new creations, as children of God.

---

[3] *Inkulturasi Liturgi,* buku kenangan Konggres Liturgi III, Jakarta, 8-13 Juli 1980, disusun oleh Sekretariat PWI Liturgi, diterbitkan oleh Dokpen MAWI, Jakarta 1980.

[4] Ir. MANGUNWIDJAJA, "Mencari bangunan gereja di Jawa Tengah", in:

The healthy community will feel and experience that "We are called to do something in this world". Just as the Church has been giving special interest to *socio-economic problems* since the beginning of her history, so also is the Church in Indonesia.[5] We

M.P.M. Muskens, *Sejarah Gereja Katolik Indonesia* 4, Ende-Flores, 1973, 190-199. For example, the Church in the village of Tambran, South Yogyakarta:

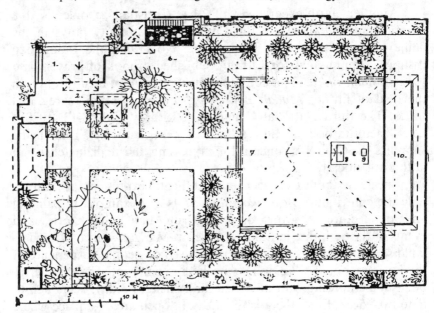

1. Entrance
2. Gate and "screen" (protecting wall)
3. "Palerepan": room for meditation in front of the Blessed Sacrament
4. Hut for forgiveness
5. Tower for signal ("Menara Kentongan")
6. Place for baptism
7. "Pendopo" = front veranda, auditorium
8. Altar
9. Pulpit
10. Sacristy
11. Wall for the way of the cross
12. Marian chapel
13. Garden for many uses (parish council, youth activities etc.)
14. Store room

[5] See J. Hadiwikarta Pr., *Himpunan Keputusan MAWI* 1924-1980, Jakarta 1981 (Obor), 49-52.

find here and there some explicitly conscious effort for socio-economic apostolate such as credit unions, community organization, conscientization of workers without forming them into institutional organizations, and so on. The socio-economic development commission of the Indonesian Bishops' Conference gives training to priests, religious and lay people for the socio-economic apostolate. We find also units of small religious communities among the people. There is a tendency to build new to build new apostolic works in the villages among the ordinary people.

Among conscious efforts toward inculturation, it is good to note *theological teaching*.[6] In the seminar on inculturation held in Jerusalem June 16-26, 1981, C.B. Putranto SJ presented a certain method of theological teaching adopted at the Institute of Philosophy and Theology in Yogyakarta. Here I want to present again his reflection on that method:

a) Not primarily a handing-over of information by the professor to the student, it is instead, a *process of theological reflection* on a given theme by the students together with a team of professors.

b) The reflection starts from the present and concrete situation of the faithful, rather than from past treatments of a topic. The present situation of the faithful includes, for example, the way they live and understand penance and forgiveness, suffering and death, expectation for salvation, etc. The students gain access to this reality by spending a couple of days in a kind of field-participant-observation situation, in which they record all the information received from the people and from their own personal experiences in encountering this reality. Then, all the experiences which have been gathered together are brought to the subsequent stage of reflection, namely, the classification and systematization of basic problems and questions. At this stage the students work together to formulate those problems in such a way as to bring out their theological relevance. This is done, for instance, by comparing them with basic philosophical questions on man, questions which contain a certain amount of abstraction. Once this is done, the students are ready for

---

[6] See T. JACOBS, "Pembaharuan dalam teologi dan dalam pengajaran teologi", in: *Orientasi* XII, 1980, 50-90 + lampiran.

the next step, namely, a dialogue and consultation with the Christian Tradition (Holy Scripture, The History of Liturgy and Theology, etc.). At this Stage these questions are handled in a deeper way, put into a wider context, clarified or answered with the help of sound hermeneutics. The next step is to reconsider the results of this investigation into the Church's Tradition as seen in the context of the experiences as originally formulated. The main question of this "confrontation" is: "in what way does the Christian Tradition answer or clarify these problems?" To find the links between the Tradition and the concrete pastoral situations is really one of thre most crucial points of the whole process. It can be mentioned in passing that another crucial point is that of the previous stage, namely, formulating the theological questions from a mass of concrete experiences taken from the observations. The final stage of this process is to formulate these links in such a way as to provide some hints for pastoral orientation or some proposal for concrete steps that are to be taken in order to improve the life of faith of the believers. Thus, these pastoral steps are founded on a theological reflection which, in turn, has started from concrete reality.

c) The subject who makes the reflection is the student. By virtue of his being a member of the Church, he does not stand as an outsider in regard to the other believers. However, he has a special function, i.e. as a future priest. The materials on which the reflection is made are the concrete reality of faith lived by the Church in a given time and place and the teaching of the Church's Tradition on a certain theme. Selected reading materials are made available to help the students to get deeper into the subject.

d) It seems that the principal aim of this method is more to foster a basic *pastoral attitude* among those future priests than to produce individuals with much theoretical knowledge of theology. A pastor, thus conceived, is expected to carry on a continuous dialogue between the actual faith of the Church living in his flock and the faith of the Church as recorded and handed down through her Tradition. In that way he leads the faithful into progress and maturity in their life of faith. This presupposes a certain level of knowledge and familiarity with both the Tradition and the concrete life of the local Church. This problem of the faithful is also his own in a deep and personal way.

Some theological principles that underlie all these proceedings seem to be the following:

1) A living faith is found not only in the documents of the past but also and firstly in the present life of the Church. Concretely, it is found in the practice and understanding of Christians, in their doubts and beliefs and in their questionings and convictions. Between the present faith and the faith of the Apostolic Church as expressed, preserved and handed down through Tradition lies a homogeneity and continuity worked by the Holy Spirit.

2) Theology serves as a reflection on faith, both the present and that expressed by Tradition, and has the task of explicity underlining the continuity and the homogenity between them. Then, this "bringing-into-consciousness" of faith should, in turn, improve the life of faith itself.

Therefore, the various branches of theology as a science with all their scientific rigor and requirements do not lose their significance. Instead, they regain their proper function in an integral way within the life of the Church. Besides, this method opens up the eyes of the students to the fact that for pastoral activities based on theological reflection open collaboration and help from other disciplines (sociology, psychology, anthropology, philosophy, etc.) are needed. For the students, the materials from the Christian Tradition can become something alive, because they are put into a living context, in a given place and time.

Not all courses use the same method. Some are held in conventional manner (lectures), some the method presented above, some course are done in a team. For example, one professor may bring to the process his own biblical reflection; another the historical, dogmatic reflection; and someone else may try to bring his contextualizing systematic reflection. The main idea here is that theological reflection begins with experience and then proceeds back to concrete experience.

2. Inculturation: Term and Concern

In the experience indicated above may be called "inculturation", then the term "inculturation" expresses *the concern*

*of the basic ecclesial community or of the local church to understand
and to live out the Gospel of Jesus Christ in a certain culture in a
concrete situation.* Christians enlivened by the Holy Spirit give
witness to their faith in Jesus Christ. They deepen their
understanding about Him not only intellectually · but also
existentially through that communication of faith which takes place
in the basic (local) group or functional group. The Gospel of Jesus
Christ is also inculturated through different kinds of artistic
expression centering on worship. Inculturation happens then in all
activities of the Christian people in their concrete surroundings. It is
not in the first instance a theoretical program. Inculturation
happens if the christian community lives and moves. Inculturation is
in the first instance *christian life* itself.

The same understanding of inculturation comes out if we
investigate the use of this term in official Church documents. Pope
John Paul II in his apostolic exhortation *Catechesi Tradendae*
(October 16, 1979) uses the term "inculturation" in the context of
the embodiment of the Gospel message in cultures.

> "As I said recently to the members of the Biblical Commission:
> 'The term 'acculturation' of '*inculturation*' may be a neologism, but it
> express very well *one factor* of the great mystery of the Incarnation'.
> (quemadmodum ad sodales Commissionis Biblicae diximus,
> *vocabulum Gallicum acculturation* vel *inculturation*' est quidem
> verbum novum, quod tamen *unum ex elementis* magni mysterii
> Incarnationis egregie exprimit') We can say of catechesis, as well as
> of evangelization in general, that it is called *to bring the power of the
> Gospel into the very heart of culture and cultures.* For this purpose,
> catechesis will seek to know these cultures and their essential
> components; it will learn their most significant expression; it will
> respect their particular values and riches. In this manner it will be
> able to offer these cultures the knowledge of the hidden mystery and
> help them to bring forth from their own living tradition original
> expressions of Christian life, celebration and thought".[7]

Later (see no. 4) we will try to understand more closely what
"one factor of the great mystery of the Incarnation" should mean.

---

[7] Pope John Paul II, *Catechesi Tradendae, apostolic exhortation on catechesis
in our time,* London 1981 (Catholic Truth Society), 68-69; *AAS* 71 (1979),
1319-1320.

Now we want just to investigate the main concern expressed in the term "inculturation". Whatever "one factor" means, the main concern of catechesis as well as of evangelization in general is "to bring the power of the Gospel into the very heart of culture and cultures". Christians of any culture should understand and live out the Gospel of Jesus Christ.

The Synod of Bishops 1977 on Catechesis had already used the term "inculturation". Again here the concern is that the christian message be rooted in the human cultures, so that the human cultures can really be accepted and transformed. The Synod points to what Vatican Council II and Pope Paul VI in his apostolic exhortation "Evangelii Nuntiandi" put forward (see GS 53, EN 19,20). Fr. Arrupe was present in that Synod. He spoke about catechesis and inculturation. What is inculturation in catechesis?

> "It is a practical corollary of the theological principle that Christ is the only Savior and that He only saves what He assumes. Consequently He should assume into His Body — which is the Church — all cultures. Naturally, purifying them of whatever may be opposed to the Holy Spirit, and in the same process saving them without destroying them. It is the penetration of faith down to the deepest levels of the life of man, effectively touching his way of thinking, feeling, and acting as a result of the animating influence of the Holy Spirit. It is offering the possibility of equal service of the Gospel to all cultural values. It is a continual dialogue between the Word of God and the many ways men have of expressing themselves. Inculturation, therefore, enables us to speak with (and not only speak to) the men and women of today about their problems and needs, their hopes and their values".[8]

P. Arrupe speaks explicitly about the Holy Spirit, the animating influence of the Holy Spirit. Christ Savior and the Word of God becomes the center of inculturation. It is good to notice how

---

[8] P. ARRUPE SJ, "Catechesis and Inculturation, The October 6 Intervention", in: *Teaching All Nations* 15 (1978), 21-24, here: 23. Cfr. what Pope Paul VI said: "Strata of humanity which are transformed: for the Church it is a question not only of preaching the Gospel in ever wider geographic areas or to ever greater members of people, but also of affecting and as it were upsetting, through the power of the Gospel, mankind's criteria of judgment, determining values, points of interest, lines of thought, sources of inspiration and models of life, which are in contrast with the Word of God and the plan of salvation" (EN 19).

P. Arrupe stresses the plurality of cultures, even all cultures and all cultural values.

The inculturation process takes place in a "dialogue of cultures" (CT 53). There are always three contexts where cultures are experienced and each context is pluralistic.[9] The first context is "the Biblical world or, more concretely, the cultural milieu in which Jesus of Nazareth lived" (CT 53). The second is the traditional context; it is the context of cultures in which the Gospel message "has already been expressed down through the centuries" (CT 53). This traditional context is also pluralistic, not only in the sense that ecumenical dialogue is included, but also dialogue within the Catholic Church itself. The third is the contemporary local context, which is obviously pluralistic and it is never in the strict sense contemporarily or locally isolated, since there is always transcultural influence.

The term inculturation expresses the concern of the basic ecclesiastical community or of the local church to understand and to live out the Gospel in a certain culture in a concrete situation. The universal Church becomes real not only through universal leaders but also through the basic ecclesial communities and local Churches, which carry out their mission. Inculturation is a new term for an old concern. It happens under His promise: I am with you always, even to the ends of time (Mt 28:20). It pervades the entire history of the Church.

3. *Theological Reflection in the Process of Inculturation*

Inculturation as described above is primarily more practical than theoretical. It is the *christian praxis,* the christian life and acts. In that praxis theological reflection should have a supporting role — hopefuly not a distorting role. The place of our theological reflection in the inculturation process can be seen in the following scheme.[10]

---

[9] E.G. Singgih in his book *Dari Israel ke Asia,* Jakarta 1982 (BPK Gunung Mulia) gives a very good contribution in reflecting on the contextualization process. There are three contexts to be noticed: the biblical context, the traditional-systematic context and the contemporary local context.

[10] Cfr. J. Holland, P. Henriot SJ, *Social Analysis; Linking Faith and Justice,*

It is true that the process of inculturation takes place by itself in any case, wherever faith is alive. But inculturation is human praxis; it includes all human abilities where reflective experience has its place and role. Theological reflection on the experience of praxis has its particular concerns and problems. Those practicing theological reflection in concrete situations may very well be helped by social sciences as, for example, sociology and anthropology. Social sciences help us to understand and to interpret the praxis, to select concerns and problems belonging to the praxis. Here we see the need of an interdisciplinary approach to reach a deeper and more critical reflection.

What is the relationship between these social sciences and theological reflection? We might see this as a distinction between "human milieu" and "divine milieu". Both are one reality, the human world in relationship to God. "Human milieu" indicates the human person and the human world as far as they are empirically approachable, as far as man is free and capable of accepting or rejecting God. "Divine milieu" indicates a reality of faith which is not capable of proof empirically. It is the reality that the human world depends on God, that the revelation of God in Jesus Christ is not just a prolongation of human capabilities. No science is able to grasp and to explain this reality fully. The special contribution of theology is to grasp and to explain realities from the experience of God's revelation. This critical theology will confront the concern and problem of christian praxis with apostolic witness. Theology needs help from social sciences. Theology is neither a "super science" above other sciences nor "pious conclusions" dictated by them.

The unifying factor of this critical reflection in an interdisciplinary approach is the praxis itself. The approach and analysis from different points of view must aim at convergence where the next praxis is planned. The commitment for the next praxis does not close the reflection; it opens it for the new experience which invites again the critical reflection. In that manner theological reflection becomes a creative contribution to inculturation, which is Christian praxis itself.

Washington 1980 (Center of Concern), 3-12; T. Jacobs SJ, "Pembaharuan dalam teologi dan dalam pengajaran teologi" in: *Orientasi* XII (1980), 50-90 + lampiran.

4. *Pneumatological Presupposition of Inculturation: The Holy Spirit in the Church and in the World's Cultures*

A pneumatological approach to inculturation-process pays a special attention to the operation of the Holy Spirit. If Pope John Paul II wrote that the term "inculturation" expresses very well one factor of the great mystery of incarnation (CT 53), this "one factor" can not be other than the work of the Holy Spirit, the same Spirit who was active in the moment of incarnation and in the Church now. In the incarnation the eternal Word became man and this was a unique happening and will never be repeated. To base inculturation directly on incarnation is not enough; it is too "far" and can bring only suggestive statements but not operational ones. We have also to take into account the presence of Holy Spirit who is outpoured in us through the cross and the resurrection.[11]

The Holy Spirit Communicates to us the mystery of the Incarnation. There are two aspects in this function of the Holy Spirit. The first aspect is the Holy Spirit in Jesus Christ and the second is now in the Church. W. Kasper describes the role of the Holy Spirit in the whole life of Jesus:

> "According to the testimony of Scripture, the Incarnation, like Jesus' whole history and fate, took place 'in the Holy Spirit'. Scripture sees the Spirit at work at all stages of Jesus' life. Jesus is conceived by the power of the Spirit by the Virgin Mary (Lk 1.35; Mt 1.18,20); at his baptism he is installed in his messianic office by the Spirit (Mk 1.10 par.); he acts in the power of the Spirit (Mk 1.12; Mt 12.28; Lk 4.14,18 et passim); on the cross, he offers himself in the Holy Spirit to the Father as victim (Heb 9.14); raised from the dead in the power of the Spirit (Rom 1.4; 8.11), he himself becomes a 'life-giving spirit' (1 Cor 15.45). The Spirit is, as it were, the medium in which God graciously acts in and through Jesus Christ and in which Jesus Christ by willing obedience is the response in personal form. Because Jesus is anointed with the Spirit (cf. Is 61.6; Lk 4.21, Acts 10.38), he is the Christ; that is, the anointed. Furthermore, it is in the Spirit that Jesus is the Son of God. Luke expresses this with unusual precision: because Jesus is in a unique way created by the power of the Spirit, 'therefore (*dio*) the child to be born will be

---

[11] Cfr. paper of Fr. A. ARIJ ROEST CROLLIUS in this seminar.

90

called... the Son of God' (Lk 1.35). Jesus' conception by the Holy Spirit (virgin birth) and his divine sonship, are therefore much more closely connected than is usually assumed".[12]

According to the second aspect the Holy Spirit is given to those who believe in Jesus Christ after His glorification (cfr. Jo 7:39; 16:7). Now the Holy Spirit is living and working in the Church, the people who believe in Jesus Christ. H. Mühlen describes the Church as the mystery of the identity of the Holy Spirit in the history of salvation, that is in Christ and in the Christians.[13] The Holy Spirit lives in the Church. We experience the Holy Spirit through the Church's life and activities.

Peter's sermon at Pentecost states that the Holy Spirit can be seen and be heard. Of course what people can see and hear is first of all the works, the effects of the Holy Spirit, but the Holy Spirit himself is really poured out. Jesus Christ — "being therefore exalted at the right hand of God, and having received from the Father the promise of the Holy Spirit, he has poured out this which you see and hear" (Acts 2:32f.).

The experience of the Holy Spirit happens through His work, through His gifts. There are varieties of gifts, but the same Spirit (1 Cor 12:4). To each is given the manifestation of the Spirit for the common good (1 Cor 12:7), for building up the Church (1 Cor 14:12). In the communication of faith where the gifts of the Spirit are communicated to one another, in the brotherhood of Christians, the Holy Spirit is experienced.

The outpouring of the Holy Spirit is linked with hearing the witness about Jesus Christ. "While Peter has still saying this, the Holy Spirit fell on all who heard the word" (Acts 10:44). And the Jewish believers who came with Peter were amazed, "because the gift of the Holy Spirit had been poured out even-on the Gentiles" (Acts 10:45).

---

[12] W. KASPER, *Jesus the Christ,* London (Burns and Oates), New York (Paulist Press), 1977, 251; originally: *Jesus der Christus,* Mainz (Matthias- Grünewald), 299.

[13] H. MÜHLEN, *Una Mystica Persona,* Die Kirche als das Mysterium der heilsgeschichtlichen Identität des heiligen Geistes in Christus und den Christen: Eine Person in vielen Personen; Paderborn [3]1968 (Schöningh). For the presentation and valuation of Mühlen's pneumatology, see: J.B. BANAWIRATMA, *Der Heilige Geist in der Theologie von Heribert Mühlen,* Frankfurt a.M. 1981 (Peter D. Lang).

The Acts of the Apostles narrates also that the experience of the Holy Spirit happens during the people's prayer in the name of Jesus. "And when they had prayed, the place in which they were gathered was shaken; and they were all filled with the Holy Spirit and spoke the word of God with boldness" (Acts 4:31). In the liturgical celebration, the celebration of the *memoria Jesu*, the Church's prayer in the name of Jesus, the gift of the Holy Spirit is experienced or renewed.

The liturgical celebration is the celebration of the *memoria Jesu*, His death and His resurrection. Jesus gives his life for our salvation, Jesus came not to be served but to serve, and to give his life as a ransom for many (Mk 10:45). In the attitude of Thanksgiving the Christian people who believe in Jesus Christ live in brotherhood (*koinonia*). They give witness about Jesus Christ (*martyria*), they celebrate what they believe and proclaim (*leitourgia*) and they are moved to serve the people in a social commitment (*diakonia*). The coming and the experience of the Holy Spirit are linked with the fundamental functions of the Church: *koinonia, martyria, leitourgia* and *diakonia*.[14]

The Holy Spirit in the Church is not like a bird in a cage. The Holy Spirit is free, the work of the Holy Spirit can not be limited by the organisational form of the Church. The Holy Spirit works also in the world, in the cultural and religious traditions which are not professing the name of Jesus Christ. The pastoral constitution *Gaudium et Spes* affirms this in a clear statement: "For since Christ died for all, and since all men are in fact called to one and the same destiny, which is divine, we must hold that the Holy Spirit offers to all the possibility of being made partners, in a way known to God, in the paschal mystery" (GS 22). The pastoral constitution speaks about "mutual relationship of Church and world" (GS 40). The Church not only offers something to the world but also receives something from the modern world (GS 44). Fr. Dupuis in his relection on The Holy Spirit and World Religions reminds us:

> "The Pastoral Constitution *Gaudium et Spes* thus ends up with what may be considered as the *magna charta* of religious dialogue between Christians and non-Christians. Religious dialogue must be

---

[14] Cfr. F. KLOSTERMANN, *Wie wird unsere Pfarrei eine Gemeinde?*, Freiburg 1979 (Herder), 27-32.

based on the recognition of the active presence of the Holy Spirit in others; it consists in a common discernment of the promptings of the Spirit experienced by all; it tends to a common action directed to build up on earth, in hope and through the Spirit, a universal brotherhood of men (and women) in God, which announces, however imperfectly, the completion of God's family in the heavenly Kingdom".[15]

We can schematize our pneumatological presupposition of inculturation-process, that is, the Holy Spirit in the Church and in the world's cultures as follows.

5. Christological Presupposition of Inculturation: Jesus Christ and His Mission as the Center of the Inculturation-Process

As we can see from the scheme above, the Holy Spirit brings the Church and the world to Christ and through Christ to "Abba", dear Father. It is the function of the Holy Spirit to unite the Son with the Father, to unite Christians with one another and with the Son.[16] Through the gift of the Holy Spirit Christians really become children of God. "When we cry 'Abba! Father!' it is the Spirit himself bearing witness with our Spirit that we are children of God, and if children, heirs, heirs of God and fellow heirs with Christ" (Rom 8:15f.). Through the Spirit, the one and the same Spirit who was in Jesus the Son, Christians participate in the life of sonship.

The participation in the life of the Son is at the same time the participation in His Mission. The Church essentially has a missionary character.[17] The mission of Jesus the Son — which is inseparable from His anointing with the Holy Spirit — is clearly formulated in Lk 4:18f. "The Spirit of the Lord is upon me, because

---

[15] J. Dupuis, "The cosmic influence of the Holy Spirit and the Gospel message" in: *God's Word Among Men*, edited by G. Gispert-Sauch, New Dehli 1973 (Vidyajyoti), 117-138, here: 133.

[16] H. Mühlen, *Der Heilige Geist als Person in der Trinität, bei der Incarnation und im Gnadenbund*: Ich – Du – Wir, Münster ³1968 (Aschendorff).

[17] W. Kasper, "Die Kirche als Sakrament des Geistes", in: W. Kasper – G. Sauter, *Kirche – Ort des Geistes*, Freiburg 1976 (Herder), 45.

he has anointed me to preach good news to the poor. He has sent me to proclaim release to the captives and recovering of sight to the blind, to set at liberty those who are oppressed, to proclaim the acceptable year of the Lord. "Luke presents Jesus in the tradition of Deutero-Isaiah as someone who brings good news at the expected time. "Today this scripture has been fulfilled in your hearing" (Lk 4:21). Jesus is someone who has to come (cfr. Lk 7:18-23). His mission is to proclaim the good news to the poor and to set the people free, He is to tell the people that God is drawing near.

Who are the poor? J. Moltmann in his reflection on the Gospel for the poor gives an explanation like this:

> "What 'poverty' means, extends from economic, social and physical -poverty to psychological, moral and religious poverty. The poor are all those who have to endure acts of violence and injustice without being able to defend themselves. The poor are all who have to exist physically and spiritually on the fringe of death, who have nothing to live for and to whom life has nothing to offer. The poor are all who are at the mercy of others, and who live with empty and open hands. Poverty therefore means both dependency and openness. We ought not to confine 'poverty' in religious terms to the general dependence of men on God. But it cannot be interpreted in a merely economic or physical sense either. It is an expression which describes the enslavement and dehumanization of man in more than one dimension. The opposite of the poor in the Old Testament is the man of violence who oppresses the poor, forces them into poverty and enriches himself at their expense".[18]

The spirituality of poverty opens the Church to Christ and to the poor. The poor are then not the object of christian virtues. The solidarity of the Church with the poor means to meet Jesus Christ, to be with Him, who identified Himself with the needy (cfr. Mt 25:31-46). Inculturation which joins together with evangelization is therefore a process of "mystical" experience, the union with Christ and of "political" commitment, solidarity with the poor. The commitment for justice, liberation, development and peace in the

---

[18] J. MOLTMANN, *The Church in the Power of the Spirit, A Contribution to Messianic Ecclesiology,* London 1977 (SCM Press), 79; originally: *Kirche in der Kraft des Geistes,* München 1975 (Kaiser), 97.

world may not be ignored in the inculturation and evangelization-process. Otherwise the Church will miss the message of the Gospel to love our neighbour who is suffering and in need (cfr. En 31). Pope John Paul II in his encyclical *Laborem Exercens* on human work sees the commitment of the Church for the workers as "a proof of her fidelity to Christ, so that she can truly be the 'Church of the poor'." (LE 8).

A pneumatological approach to inculturation leads to the center of the whole process, that is, Jesus Christ and his mission. The basic ecclesial communities, the local Churches, become then the experience of Christ's presence among them as the center of their life.

6. *Some Pastoral Insights and Orientations*

6.1. Our pneumatological approach to inculturation is centered in Christian praxis. It is an approach through the experience of the Church, in which the Holy Spirit is living and working. From the praxis-experience we draw our faith-concern and then confront this with the apostolic witness. After this confrontation the commitment for the next stage can be planned. Our pneumatological approach follows the process: experience — concern — theological reflection — commitment for the next step. This process should become a process of discernment, it begins with the experience of the Holy Spirit and should be conduced by the same Spirit. This inculturation-process should be characterized by readiness for conversion. The process of discernment has a critical and creative character with regard to the praxis.

6.2. In that process the basic ecclesial community or the local Church is trying to understand and to live out the Gospel of Jesus Christ in a certain culture in a concrete situation. The inculturation-process joins together with the evangelization. It happens in four fundamental functions of the Church: "koinonia", "martyria", "leitourgia" and "diakonia".

6.3. In this process the Church is closely united with Jesus Christ and His mission. The function of the Holy Spirit is to bring the people as children of God to communion with Christ and His mission. The readiness for mission characterizes the inculturation-process. Christians participate in the life of the Son and in His mission. Christian life is characterized by these two elements: communion with Christ and commitment for the poor.

6.4. Therefore the spirituality of the Church has a twofold fidelity: fidelity to Christ and to the people we serve.[19] We serve the people as a sign of our fidelity to Christ and we serve them as Christ did and does now in the Holy Spirit.

6.5. Since the Holy Spirit may not be limited by the ecclesiastical organization, the Church has to be sensitive to the life and the work of the Holy Spirit in other religious traditions and in the world's cultures. The work of the Holy Spirit brings people to communion with one another and with God. No good tree bears bad fruit nor does a bad tree bear good fruit, each tree is known by its own fruit (cf. Llk 7:43f.). We could follow St. Paul by noticing the fruits of the Holy Spirit; the fruits of the Spirit are "love, joy, peace, patience, kindness, goodness, faithfulness, gentleness, self control" (Gal 5:22f.).

6.6. The guarantee of the inculturation-process is the Holy Spirit Himself. In Him we may keep our hope, "and hope does not disappoint us, because God's love has been poured into our hearts through the Holy Spirit which has been given to us" (Rom 5:5).

J.B. Banawiratma, S.J.

---

[19] Cfr. Pope Paul VI: "This fidelity both to a message whose servants we are and to the people to whom we must transmit it living and intact is the central axis of evangelization" (EN 4).

Maria Elena Chiong-Javier

RELIGION AS ENTRY POINT TO CHANGE AND DEVELOPMENT: THE CASE OF THE HANUNUO MANGYAN *

* The author acknowledges the assistance of the De La Salle University-Research Center in the preparation of this paper, particularly of Mr. Ruben Z. Martinez, researcher, who helped in gathering field data. She is most indebted to the Hanunuo residents of Bait, the Sisters of Siervas de San Jose, and Fr. Antoon Postma, S.V.D., without whose cooperation this paper would not have been possible.

97

It has been the experience of many a culture that religion is a potent medium of change. In the case of the Philippines, over four hundred years ago, the introduction of Christianity resulted in the modification of not only the religious but also the social, economic, and political aspects of the native Filipino culture. The Spanish missionaries who first came to christianize the Filipinos were not restricted to the practice of their church roles; they played quite active parts as linguists, ethnologists, educators, estate administrators, and public officials. Hence they affected almost every facet of community life.

Since then lowland Filipino missionaries have gradually taken over the task of living and preaching among the non-Christian Filipinos, of whom many comprise the so-called indigenous, tribal, or ethnic minority groups. These groups generally reside in the mountainous recesses of the country. And oftentimes, their initial contacts with fellow Filipinos from the lowland majority groups from whom they have grown apart over the centuries are made through the missionaries who are themselves lowlanders. The missionaries' orientation toward service to the poor and the needy has led them to effect changes for the betterment of indigenous peoples.

This paper seeks to describe the major changes that have occurred among the Hanunuo (or Hanunoo) Mangyan — an ethnic minority group inhabiting the foothills of Mansalay in Mindoro Oriental, Philippines — as a result of the missionary work undertaken among them by a group of Sisters belonging to the Catholic religious congregation of Siervas de San Jose (Servants of St. Joseph).[1] Initially, the paper presents some background information on the Hanunuo Mangyan of Mindoro Island. Then it describes Bait (Bah-eet), the settlement of the Hanunuo concerned

---

[1] Field data for this paper were obtained through participant observation, an anthropological method, which was conducted in Bait for a total period of one month in early 1985.

in this paper, and the Sisters' Mission in and around Bait. This is followed by a discussion of the modifications that the Sisters' Mission have ushered into the Hanunuo's traditional beliefs and/or practices pertaining to three cultural aspects, namely religion, health and healing, and economic life. The paper concludes with some implications for missionary work in indigenous cultures which have been drawn from the Sisters' experiences in Bait.

THE HANUNUO MANGYAN OF MINDORO

The term "Mangyan" is a generic name for the proto-Malayan minority groups inhabiting the mountains and foothills of Mindoro, the seventh largest island in the Philippines. Based on linguistic affinities, the Mangyan have been classified into two broad groupings: (1) the northern group composed of the Iraya, Alangan, and Tadyawan; and (2) the southern group comprised of the Hanunuo, Buhid, and Batangan (Tweddell, 1970; Lopez, 1976; Barbian, 1979; Lamberte, 1983). The southern group, according to Lopez (1976), is culturally more advanced as evidenced by its technological achievements (e.g., pottery-making and loom- weaving) and pre-Hispanic form of syllabary. This group has been also adequately studied. In addition one of its members, the Hanunuo, is the most extensively described Mangyan group (Lamberte, 1983).[2]

The Hanunuo occupy a 800-square-kilometer area located in the hinterlands of the southern municipalities of Mindoro Island: Mansalay and Bulalacao in Mindoro Oriental, and Magsaysay and San Jose in Mindoro Occidental. Reported estimates on their population are varied, but tended generally to cluster around figures ranging from 5,000 to 7,000 (Lamberte, 1983). Various studies have revealed that the Hanunuo address themselves as "Mangyan" to mean man, tribesman, or mountain inhabitant or as "Hanunuo Mangyan" to denote real or genuine Mangyan (see also Lamberte, 1983).

---

[2] In a study of contemporary Mangyan researches, LAMBERTE (1983) found out that many of the accounts on the Hanunuo characteristics could be traced to studies undertaken by Fr. Antoon POSTMA and Fr. Emeterio DE LA PAZ of the S.V.D. Catholic Missionary Congregation.

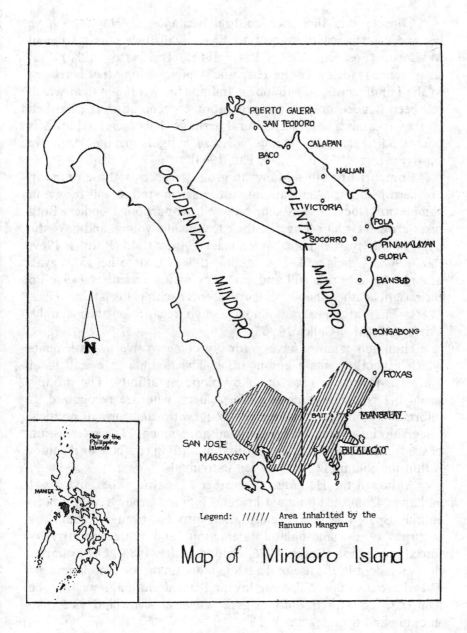

Legend: ////// Area inhabited by the Hanunuo Mangyan

Map of Mindoro Island

101

Conscious of their rich cultural heritage, the Hanunuo have become assertive with respect to being a distinct ethnic tribe in Mindoro (Postma, 1965; Paz, 1968; Lamberte, 1983). Of significance is their own pre-Hispanic syllabic writing that is related to the Hindu script still found in India. This writing system which has been handed down from generation to generation is cherished by the group as a valuable cultural heritage. It is preserved in their poetry, particularly the famous *ambahan,* a highly metaphorical love song (Postma, 1965 and 1981; Paz, 1968).[3]

Compared to other Mangyan groups especially those found in northern Mindoro, the Hanunuo are taller in stature and brown in complexion; they possess slim but well proportioned bodies. Both sexes grow their hair long, file their teeth while young, and have the habit of chewing betel nuts which blacken their teeth (Postma, 1969; Paz, 1968; Garcia, 1973; Conklin, 1958). Like other Mangyan groups, they are peaceful and shy; they would retreat and give up their rights rather than stand up to encroaching lowlanders (Paz, 1968). They also generally show a high regard for their family, elders, and tribe (Callejo, 1963).

Hanunuo families have gradually come to live in settlements which generally remain autonomous. The families in a settlement are often related to each other by blood or affinity. The group's social life is family-centered. Their elders, who are recognized as informal community leaders, co-exist with the formal political leadership influenced by the national government. The intercession of the former is normally sought first in settling conflicts or disputes within the community or between individuals.

Although the Hanunuo, like other Mangyan tribes, live apart and away from the dominant lowland Filipinos, they have not been entirely spared of the acculturation process brought about by centuries of lowland-upland interaction, and more recently, by forced integration (Lopez, 1976; Chiong-Javier, 1984). For example, they are adept in the use of Tagalog, a dominant lowland language. They have also adapted some lowland-styled clothing (such as the t-shirt) to go with traditional garb, as well as lowland vices like smoking and drinking alcohol.

---

[3] Fr. Postma, who has taken an intensive interest in the Hanunuo while doing missionary work among them, now possesses a rich and extensive collection of personal researches on the ambahan and other forms of Hanunuo folklore.

The Hanunuo's primary economic activity is still subsistence agriculture (see next section for a lengthier discussion). Hence, land to the Hanunuo is an important commodity. It has also become, over the years, a basic problem shared by all Mangyan groups and by other Philippine tribal communities as well. Kaingin farms left to fallow are taken over by lowlanders; ancestral domains including forests, settlements, or reservation areas are encroached upon by migrants and multi-national corporations engaged in logging and agri-business. This problem has gained significance because it not only disrupts their social and economic life, but also impairs their socioeconomic development (Jacinto, 1977; Leykamm, 1980; OTRADEV, 1980; Chiong-Javier, 1984).

Life for the Hanunuo, like other upland peoples, is generally characterized by poverty and its accompanying ills: high mortality and morbidity, rampant malnutrition because of poor diet and food shortage, low level of literacy, and lack of access to adequate services (Sevilla, 1982). Particularly in recent years, this plight of the uplanders have been the focus of both government and non-government agencies, including religious groups which appear to be especially drawn to them and to have had a longer record of working among them.

THE BAIT COMMUNITY

Bait is one of the 22 sitios under the jurisdiction of Panaytayan, the only barangay found in Mansalay that is predominantly populated by the Hanunuo Mangyan.[4] (Mansalay is located 281 kilometers south of Manila, the former capital of the Philippines). Bait is also the only sitio in the barangay that is most accessible from the Poblacion (town center) of Mansalay, hence it was chosen as a mission base for the St. Joseph Sisters. It is located about 8 kilometers from the Poblacion and can be reached through any one of the buses and jeepneys that ply that provincial highway connecting Mansalay to the next town of Bulalacao (at the southernmost tip of Mindoro Oriental) or the tricycles that bring

---

[4] A barangay is the smallest political unit in the Philippines. It is synonymous to village or barrio.

passengers from the Poblacion to the nearby barangays. While the rider may hire the tricycle to take him directly to Bait, he will have to alight from the bus or jeepney at a highway junction and hike some 3 kilometers over a rough road traversing the Kagankan River to reach the sitio.

Located at the base of a mountain range, Bait provides both entry to and exit from a number of less accessible upland Hanunuo settlements found amidst forested areas. The sitio itself is characterized by uneven terrain with the secondary forests and *kaingin* (slash-and-burn or swidden agriculture) farms serving as a backdrop. The rough road which connects Bait to the provincial highway ends in the heart of the sitio; some portions which traverse the rivers before Bait become impassable or washed out during the rainy season (June to November). There is also a concrete-and-wooden bridge in the sitio that leads to the church and the Sisters' house, both constructed on higher grounds.[5] The dwelling units of the Hanunuo families, which are generally made of light materials (such as bamboo and cogon grass), cluster around these structures. In addition, there are the elementary school, the library, the marketplace, the communal toilet and bath, the garage for the Sisters' vehicle, the semi-permanent house now occupied by a representative of Foster Parents' Plan,[6] and the extended building (built in phases) which contains the cooperative store, the clinic-cumdrugstore, and the new 8-bed hospital. The drinking water in Bait comes from natural mountain springs and is stored for the residents' use in three concrete tanks: one for the Sisters and two for the Hanunuo families and others. Lighting is provided by gas lamps.

The early improvements in Bait were undertaken largely through the efforts of Fr. Antoon Postma, S.V.D., who has been working among the Hanunuo Mangyan in the Panaytayan area since the late fifties. Fr. Postma extended his mission work to Bait two years after staying in Panaytayan Proper. He obtained the necessary funds from individual benefactors for the construction between 1975 and 1979 of some infrastructures (road and bridge)

---

[5] The bridge was built to facilitate access to the church grounds.

[6] The Foster Parents' Plan is a foreign-funded program addressing the welfare of children. It provides assistance especially in the areas of nutrition and education.

and buildings (church, garage, the semipermanent houses currently occupied by the Sisters and the Foster Parents' Plan representative, and a section of the extended building). The Hanunuo contributed unskilled labor during the construction. Fr. Postma, who was instrumental in setting up the Sister's Bait Mission, also facilitated the financing of later innovations introduced by the Sisters, like the clinic and the hospital. The school and the library, on the other hand, were put up primarily through funds from the government and the Foster Parents' Plan.

At present, the residents of Bait are composed of approximately 15 Hanunuo households (averaging 10 members per household, or a total population of 150 individuals), the religious community of four Sisters, a lowland Visayan family, and the social worker representing the \Foster Parents' Plan.[7] Because of the location of the sitio, there are also a small number of regular transients who usually stay there overnight on the way to or from the upper sitios. They include the United States' peace corp volunteers, the personnel of the Bureau of Forest Development which has a participatory upland development pilot project in the Malang-og region, the researchers of the De La Salle University-Research Center in charge of documenting this project, and the protestant missionaries of the Overseas Missionary Fellowship.

THE BAIT MISSION

On 7 June 1980, the Siervas de San Jose established a mission in Bait to fulfill their own evangelical work and at the same time assist Fr. Postma in helping the Hanunuo to help themselves.[8] The

---

[7] The lowland Visayan family lives in the marketplace across the river. The marketplace bustles with activity every Friday, during which both Mangyan and non-Mangyan (locally termed *damuong* or outsider) residents of surrounding areas congregate to buy and/or sell (e.g., the Mangyan sells uncooked banana to the damuong but buys cooked and sweetened banana from him). For the Mangyan, it also serves as a place for socializing and exchanging news.

[8] For one and a half years prior to the arrival of the St. Joseph Sisters, a lay missionary lived in Bait and helped with Fr. Postma's evangelical work. This Sister is now working among another Hanunuo group in the next town of Bulalacao.

Bait Mission is the congregation's only mission among the cultural minorities in the Philippines. (Their other missions are found in the rural lowland and urban economically-depressed areas).

Of the four Sisters originally assigned to the Mission, only one has remained to date; the three others had been reassigned after staying in the sitio for between two and four years. At present, there are also four Sisters with the Mission. They are: (1) Sr. Julia, one of the pioneers and a senior Sister as well as the leader of the group; (2) Sr. Virgie, who arrived in 1982; (3) Sr. Edith, who joined the group in 1984; and (4) Sr. Aurora, the youngest member who came together with Sr. Edith.[9]

The Sisters define their mission's general thrust as "insertion among the poor people in the world." In Bait, its main concern is two-pronged: the spiritual and the physical wellbeing of the Hanunuo. Thus the Sisters' major aims are to evangelize and to uplift the socioeconomic conditions of these people. In undertaking their mission work, they are guided by two things: (1) respect for the Hanunuo's indigenous culture, and (2) conscious portrayal of themselves as role models (or, as the Sisters call it, "witnessing" or "bearing witness to Christ's life").

Thus since founding the Mission, the Sisters have been preaching and teaching the Hanunuo adults and children about Catholic beliefs and ways. Their introduction of new precepts have always proceeded gradually and with due caution. The Sisters also gently but firmly and repeatedly discouraged those traditional Hanunuo practices that clash or conflict with the Christian teachings or with what they consider to be good for a person (see next section for some examples).

Because the Mission concerns the people's physical or material welfare, the Sisters have also initiated and supported a variety of projects aimed at uplifting the Hanunuo's quality of life (see Table). There are livelihood projects that are geared to improve the people's economic conditions and, more specifically, to provide them with some means of obtaining cash for basic household needs (especially goods not produced in the kaingin farms). There are health-related projects intended to enhance the people's chances of survival,

---

[9] Sr. Julia celebrated her silver anniversary as a religious nun last 3 February 1985. Sr. Aurora, in turn, will receive her perpetual vows early next year.

through sanitation, health, and nutrition education and practices, and access to lifesaving drugs and facilities. The Sisters address too the improvement of people's literacy level through their conduct of functional literacy classes for Hanunuo families living in the less accessible sitios surrounding Bait. These activities are part of the Sisters' community assistance program which is implemented with the help of trained Mangyan community workers.

Because for the past years the Sisters have lived and worked among the Hanunuo, prayed with them, and shared both their happiness and frustrations, they have gained the Hanunuo's confidence. Their firsthand knowledge of lowland systems and institutions have been most useful as they serve as the Hanunuo's intermediaries, counselors, and guardians in the latter's dealings with lowlanders.

As mentioned, the Bait Mission operates largely under the auspices of Fr. Postma. From him, the Sisters and the Hanunuo have constantly received moral guidance and support. Through him, they have derived financial assistance for the various projects of the Mission and/or community. In addition, the Sisters' own congregation and friends have likewise been supportive of the Mission by their contributions of time and money, including loans, for its projects.

SOME MAJOR INNOVATIONS INTRODUCED INTO THE HANUNUO CULTURE

Within a span of five years, the Bait Mission has apparently made the most impact on three aspects of the Hanunuo culture, namely religion, health and healing, and economic life. This impact can be seen in the changes that have been made in these aspects of the people's life.

Religion

Like other Mangyan groups, the Hanunuo traditionally believe in the existence of environmental spirits which have the power to influence or touch the lives of the living Mangyan. In particular, the spirits can cause misfortune or illness. Thus the Hanunuo find it

List of Inputs provided by the Siervas de San Jose Sisters to the Hanunuo Mangyan of Bait, Mansalay, Mindoro Oriental (June 1980 to May 1985)*

Religious/ spiritual inputs	Economic inputs	Social Welfare inputs	Community Development inputs
Catechetical instruction	Cooperative variety store	Clinic and drugstore	Active involvement of the Hanunuo who are trained as community workers
Celebration of Holy Eucharist	Samahan sa Mais	Hospital	
		Referrals to external health providers	
Observance of holy days of obligation	Beading and weaving project	Cooking classes	
Marriage enrichment seminars	Assistance in opening bank accounts and resolving land problems	Construction of communal and private latrines, and water system	
Preparations for baptism, marriage, and holy communion		Functional literacy classes	
Religion classes in school			

*The listing is not exhaustive but includes the major inputs of the Sisters.

108

necessary to determine, through the help of a local specialist (see below), the kind of spirit involved in order to be able to treat a problem.

Into the Hanunuo's traditional beliefs the Sisters introduced Catholicism by: (1) giving catechetical instructions, particularly to prepare individuals for the acceptance of certain sacraments, (2) observing the Sunday Mass and other Church celebrations like Lent and Christmas, and (3) holding marriage enrichment seminars. These activities have helped in developing the Hanunuo's understanding and acceptance of the new religion and, possibly, in incorporating this with their traditional beliefs.

Catechetical instructions. Using a combination of Hanunuo and Tagalog languages, the Sisters give religious instructions during: pre-Sunday Mass, informal meetings with the community, regular visits to outlying sitios, and religion classes in Bait Elementary School. During these occasions, they introduce the sign of the cross and the concept of God as a loving Father. The Sisters describe their approach to teaching religion as "evocative" or "experiential" rather than "doctrinal". Much of their teachings are drawn from Bible stories and related to the experiences of the Hanunuo. They stress positive values like appreciation for the person as a child of God, responsibility to oneself, one's family, and to others, sharing, caring, and living by example.

In coordination with Fr. Postma who administers the sacraments, the Sisters prepare the Hanunuo to receive these. Baptism, the sacrament initially introduced, is held twice a year: one on Easter Sunday and another during Christmas. It is administered to infants whose parents are already baptized and to children or adults who have received catechetical instructions. These instructions may extend up to as much as 6 months to enable the Sisters to explain baptism and its requirements and to observe whether the applicant is properly motivated (i.e., he wants to be baptized *not* for such reasons as to avail of free medicines or special favors from the Sisters or Fr. Postma, and he regularly attends church services). On the day before baptism, the Sisters review with the applicants the meaning of baptism and the tasks to be undertaken during the rite. The baptismal rite, which is officiated by Fr. Postma, is conducted in the Hanunuo language. It is followed by the celebration of a Mass, after which the newly christened is treated to lunch.

Again, if properly motivated, the christened Hanunuo who desires to receive the sacraments of Penance and Holy Communion also undergoes a preparatory phase handled by the Sisters. Matrimony and Extreme Unction are two sacraments that the Sisters encourage the Hanunuo faithful to receive if appropriate. In the process of preaching matrimony, they discourage the latter from marrying too young (traditionally in the early teens) and from practising the *paglalayis* or *harana* (which allows the suitor to sleep with the girl prior to marriage).

The Mass and other Church rites. The celebration of the Mass was introduced in Bait in the early sixties by Fr. Postma. The earlier masses were held in a previous chapel built by the sitio residents themselves. At present, the Mass and other religious celebrations are conducted in a larger chapel that was constructed through funds solicited by Fr. Postma.

The priest visits the community twice a week; one of his visits occurs on Sunday during which he says the Mass. Attended by about 30 to 50 people from Bait and vicinity, the Sunday Mass is celebrated in the Hanunuo language. The procedures followed are basically those observed also in the lowland Catholic Church. Fr. Postma's weekday visit (Thursday) is devoted to saying Mass for the Sisters and attending to the needs of the Mission.

The preparation of the chapel for religious services is handled by the Sisters with assistance from the Mangyan community workers. While going about their tasks in the community, they also constantly remind the people to attend the services.

Marriage Enrichment Seminars. This type of activity is undertaken by the Sisters for two reasons: to introduce the concept of the Holy Family to married couples who have been baptized and assiduous in attending the Mass, and to broaden their knowledge and understanding of married life particularly the obligations to spouse and children. The seminar is held every 19th of the month. Recently, it was attended by seven couple from Bait and nearby settlements.

Health and Healing

The Hanunuo attribute poor health or illness to the work of any of the spirits they believe in. To diagnose the cause of the ailment, they go to a traditional healer called *pamulungan* (medicine

110

man) who uses tree barks and herbs to treat the sick. If he cannot cure the sick because an evil spirit is behind the ailment, a *pandaniwan* is consulted. The latter is said to possess the power to draw out the evil spirit from the affected or ailing part of the body. The pandaniwan also prescribes the use of medicinal plants for curing.

Noting that poor health and the absence of health facilities were among the major problems of the Hanunuo in Bait, the Sisters have undertaken the following tasks since their mission was established. They have asked the people to allow not only the traditional healers but also themselves to treat the sick. They have also encouraged the Hanunuo from discontinuing certain unsanitary practices, introduced new ways, and provided access to modern medicines and facilities largely through referrals and the construction of a clinic-cum-drugstore and a hospital in the sitio. These innovations are becoming increasingly sought after and utilized by the Hanunuo as both an alternative to traditional healing methods and whenever these methods do not work.

Sanitary practices encouraged. These practices are: (1) not to spit anywhere after chewing betel nuts, (2) to wash the hands especially before handling food, (3) to wear clean clothes, and (4) to observe the proper disposal of human wastes and garbage. To complement these, the Sisters have introduced the construction of private latrines and a communal toilet-and-bath (originally intended for community guests). The latter, which the Sisters had had built, is now widely used but needs to be properly maintained by its users. They have also spearheaded the construction of a system for storing safe drinking water. In addition, Sr. Virgie conducted for one year a monthly cooking class attended by seven to 12 Hanunuo wives. Through this class, the womenfolk learned new and more nutritious ways of preparing food, particularly staple items like banana, sweet potato, and cassava.

Clinic-cum-drugstore. Before the Sisters came to Bait, Fr. Postma set up a drug depot that was open only when he was around. He later hired a Hanunuo assistant who was trained to dispense drugs for common ailments in the area like colds, fever, and malaria. The training was given by Dr. Danilo Labitan, a medical practitioner from the next town of Mansalay.[10] When Sr. Julia arrived, the

---

[10] Dr. Labitan served his rural practicum in Fr. Postma's Panaytayan

clinic-cum-drugstore was established permanently and the assistant, given a more thorough training.

The clinic depends largely on Fr. Postma for the provision of a continuous supply of drugs, although Sr. Julia manages to solicit medicines from some drug companies in Manila. It is open for 7 hours a day (8:30 a.m. to 5:oo p.m. with noon break of 1.5 hours). The current Hanunuo female assistant, who has also been trained as a community worker, takes charge of dispensing medicines from pain relievers to oral rehydration solutions. In return for these medicines, the clients donate small amounts ranging from P050 to P2.50 (approximately $0.03 to $0.14 at P18.50/dollar). This practice, according to the Sisters, serves to discourage the Hanunuo from depending on dole-outs. The clinic accumulates about P60-100 ($3.24-5.41) a month from its clients' donations. This fund is being utilized for the construction of the hospital.

Serious ailments are referred by the assistant to Sr. Julia who, in turn, refers these cases to the nearest provincial government hospital or to a Manila hospital. Sr. Julia herself accompanies the sick and settles the resulting financial obligations. The recipient or his family offers services in exchange.

Hospital. In 1981, Sr. Julia started admitting lying-in patients in a small cogon-thatched house for certain medical cases. This house gave way to a concrete hospital built adjacent to the clinic in May 1984 to March 1985. Construction costs amounting to about P111,000 ($6,000) were shouldered largely by the contributions and loans solicited by Sr. Julia from friends and benefactors of the Mission, including Fr. Postma, the Sisters congregation and the Foster Parents' Plan; a part of it (about P20,000) came from the sale of unused medical supplies from the clinic. The construction activities were undertaken by two paid skilled lowland carpenters and four Hanunuo volunteers (who worked to reciprocate the favors extended by the Sisters). The Hanunuo children who gathered stones and rocks from the river were rewarded 5 centavos apiece.

The hospital includes an 8-bed ward and a small examination room; it also has a water system. (The Sisters incurred an

---

Mission. Although based in Mansalay, he continues to take interest in the Mangyan and occasionally visits Bait to give medical assistance to the Sisters. At present he is the resident physician at the MEDICARE hospital in Roxas.

outstanding debt of P/36,000 ($1,946) for this project). The hospital opened in April 1985 and was able to admit about 20 patients after three months. These patients were confined from 3 days to a week for ailments like malaria, influenza, severe dehydration causes by gastrointestinal diseases, and tuberculosis. Sr. Julia manages the hospital with help from her clinic assistant and, occasionally, from Dr. Labitan. When not in use, the hospital doubles as a guest house while the latter's construction has yet to be completed.

Economic Life

The Hanunuo continue to depend on traditional, subsistence-based agriculture as a major source of livelihood; this is mainly supplemented by the sale of forest products and by raising livestock. Their economic life is thus inextricably linked to the kaingin farm and forest. Located on sloping land, the kaingin farms are usually planted during the wet season with a variety of crops including banana, rootcrops (mainly cassava, sweet potato, and taro), corn, upland rice, legumes and other vegetables, coconut and other fruit trees. The Hanunuo generally have more than one farm but not all are under cultivation at the same time. After using the land for about two years, it is left to fallow or to regenerate for a longer duration of as much as 5-10 years (but this period has recently been shortened because of the scarcity of farm land).

Like other upland peoples, the subsistence economy of the Hanunuo has been increasingly affected by the monetized lowland economy. To obtain money, they raise cash crops, sell surplus farm product and animals, and hire out their labor to the lowlanders. However, these economic pursuits have hardly been sufficient to augment the low agricultural productivity, a problem that plagues the majority of them. Moreover, because they only have the traditional usufruct claims on the land and possess no legal document to substantiate this claim, the loss of land due to encroachment presents a constant threat.

Cognizant of these problems, the Sisters' Mission have made way for the following activities: (1) establishment of two cooperatives — the Samahan sa Mais (literally, association for corn) and the cooperative variety store, (2) project on beading and weaving, (3) support and encouragement for the opening of individual bank accounts, and (4) linkage with non-government

113

volunteer organizations that address the land problem of minority groups.

Samahan sa Mais. Encouraged and guided by Sr. Julia, this cooperative association was formed in 1982 with the objective of marketing corn in the lowlands. Presently composed of 12 Bait residents, the association first borrowed a small amount of capital from the Sister to defray the costs of buying corn sacks and of transporting the corn to the lowlands.

Operating on the *halili* system, the association contacts a lowland buyer prior to the corn harvest and agrees on the price of corn per sack (usually determined by the buyer based on prevailing market price) and the volume to be delivered to him. The buyer, in turn, advances to the association a portion of the pre-agreed total payment. Using this advance, the association buys more corn from non-members. After the required volume has been assembled, the corn are brought to the buyer who completes the payment.

In the last corn harvest season, the association profited a sum of P 750 ($40.50) from the sale of 50 sacks of corn to its regular buyer. (The buying rate was P 130/sack or $7.03/sack). Half of the profit was equally divided among its 12 members; each member's share was P 31.25 ($1.69). The other half was retained by the association partly to be used as capital and partly to offset its outstanding debt.

Cooperative variety store. Established in August 1984, this cooperative enterprise has a current membership of 128 Hanunuo residents (two-thirds of whom come from Bait and the remainder from neighboring sitios). Each member has paid for a share worth P 100 ($5.40). In the case of Bait, the household investment in this co-op venture ranged from P 100 (for one household member) to P 700 (for seven members); the average investment per household (for 15 households in all) comes to P 300 ($16.22).

The initial amount collected from the paid-up shares were used by Sr. Julia to purchase the merchandise for the store. Then she hired a female Hanunuo storekeeper (whose family occupies the backroom of the store at no cost) who is paid from the store's income. After almost a half-year of existence, in a meeting on 3 January 1985 the cooperative through Sr. Julia distributed the first dividend equivalent to the paidup share of every member. The Sister also gave a financial status report written on the blackboard. This report indicates that in 5 months, the store grossed P 29,410.20 (about P 200/day); spent P 25,248.75; netted a profit a P 4,161.45; and had stocks on hand worth P 5,463.20. The Sister also enjoined the members to continue patronizing their store as this would redound to their benefit.

Sr. Julia has been most active in the management of the store and the supervision of its personnel's tasks (vending and record-keeping). Once a week she buys from Mansalay replenishments for such goods as candies, biscuits, dried fish and some perishable items which amount to P 50-100. Once every two months and on her journey to Manila, she purchases goods with longer shelf life (like canned food stuffs) and durable goods (beads, umbrellas, and clothes) for the store; these purchases amount to P 500-1000. Together with the co-op members she is hopeful that the small store, which is housed in Fr. Postma's former garage and located beside the clinic, will continue to flourish.

Beading and weaving project. Handled by Sr. Virgie, this project was undertaken in 1984 to enable the womenfolk to earn some cash income from home-based production of beaded and woven items. The Sister took charge of marketing their products. After a year, the project was temporarily discontinued because of a number of reasons: the high cost of raw materials supplied through the co-op store, the absence of a permanent market, the lack of interest among the Hanunuo women to pursue beading and weaving as an income-generating activity,[11] and the Sister's own hectic work schedule.

Individual bank accounts. Because the expected offshoot of their income-generating projects was an increase in the Hanunuo's cash earnings, the Sisters decided that it was also necessary for them to learn the thrift habit and the mechanics of saving in a bank. Sr. Julia, who takes charge of this program, handles the orientation of the prospective depositor, and facilitates and assists in his transactions (opening an account, depositing, and withdrawing) with the Mansalay Rural Bank. She also keeps blank slips for these transactions. According to the Bank manager, a number of Bait residents (mostly males) have deposits ranging from P 10 to about P 1,000 ($54.05).

---

[11] The Hanunuo women make beaded jewelry (bracelets, necklaces, and earrings) and weave baskets and clothing materials for either personal or household use only.

Linking up with other organizations to resolve land issues.
Knowing how important land is to the Hanunuo, the Sisters
consider this activity necessary to ensure the protection of this land
from encroachers. In order that they would be more effective in
advising and helping the Hanunuo resolve and prevent
land-grabbing problems, they have studied the legal issues affecting
these; attended seminars and workshops whenever applicable;
contacted lawyers and followed up court cases; and joined an
informal network of individuals and groups (like the paralegal
training and community organizing groups and the U.S. peace corp
volunteers) concerned with the protection of the so-called ancestral
land rights of indigenous peoples.

CONCLUSION

This case study of the Hanunuo Mangyan has demonstrated
that religion could be an effective entry point to both cultural
change and socio-economic development among the ethnic
minorities. It has indicated how the Siervas de San Jose Sisters
facilitated the Hanunuo's acculturation and integration into the
mainstream of lowland (Catholic) faith and lifeways, and improved
their living conditions through various development-oriented
projects.

The major factors that seemed to have accounted for the
Sisters' effectiveness as innovators or change agents are as follows.
One, being a religious group the Sisters are highly motivated in
and deeply committed to their work among the poor and
underprivileged minorities. This is generally the people's perception
of them which they have been reinforcing by example. Two, the
Sisters possess the ability to not only identify but also immediately
address the more pressing needs of the community such as those
problems related to health and land ownership. Three, they are also
able to harness both external and indigenous resources to meet the
goals of the community projects they have initiated. Four, their
approach to mission work is comprehensive in nature and their
activities are multi-pronged: religion and spiritually are interspersed
with community development programs. And fifth, because as
religious they tend to stay over a long period of time in the

116

community, the Sisters can ensure the continuity and sustainability of their programs and projects for the people.

The Sisters' work among the Hanunuo in Bait also point to three main considerations for the conduct of missionary activities especially among indigenous peoples. First, the Sisters manage to use with apparent effectiveness the traditional top-down approach to development work, although the viability of this approach has been questioned in other fields with the recent emergence and growing acceptability of the participatory mode or the bottom-up approach. But the accumulated experiences of those who have tried the latter mode suggest that community development efforts tend to have a more enduring effect if they actively involve the intended beneficiaries in the different aspects of planning, implementation, and evaluation. This participatory process, however, is a long and slow process. Nevertheless, the prospects for its adoption in missionary tasks seem to be great in view of the religious' ability to generate acceptance of top-down initiated activities. But this would perhaps require a drastic reorientation for most missionaries.

Second, the Sisters' experience reveals the people's willingness to respond to the Mission's needs and tasks, particularly since it has shown its concern for their well-being. But how to translate this response into a more meaningful participation that could be channeled to build self-reliance and capabilities within the community has often posed a problem to community workers in many sectors of development. The Hanunuo, through proper and adequate training from the Sisters, have emerged capable of transcending traditional capacities: they dispense medicines, manage a store and record transactions, negotiate a business deal with the lowlander, and even do organizing work. This represents a step toward developing strong, self-reliant, and viable indigenous communities.

And finally, the Hanunuo's experience has indicated the possibility of actively involving the missionary groups in national development programs addressing the concerns of highland peoples, especially in view of the resource constraints faced by implementing agencies. The missionaries themselves could, in turn, benefit from a better coordination with government and volunteer organizations whose technical expertise will be a boon to missionary work.

MARIA ELENA CHIONG-JAVIER

117

REFERENCES CITED

BARBIAN, Karl Josef (1979), The Tribal Distribution of the Mangyans *in* Philippine Culture and Society, 5:15-11.

CALLEJO, Marcelino C. (1963), A Study of the Culture of the Mangyan Tribes of Mindoro. Lyceum of the Philippines, (unpublished master's thesis). Manila.

CHIONG-JAVIER, Ma. Elena (1985), Economic Exchange between the Iraya Mangyan and the Tagalog in Mindoro Oriental, Philippines: Preliminary Notes. *In* Community Forestry: Socio-economic Aspects, edited by Y.S. Rao, N.T. Vergara, and G.W. Lovelace. Regional Office for Asia and the Pacific, Food and Agriculture Organization of the United Nations, Bangkok. Pp. 305-327.

CONKLIN, Harold C. (1958), "Betel Chewing Among the Hanunuo". Abstract No. 66, Fourth Far Eastern Prehistory Congress. Special reprint. Diliman, Quezon City: National Research Council of the Philippines, U.P.

GARCIA, Isabel L. (1973), A Study of the School Problems of the Mangyans of Southern Mindoro. Ateneo de Manila University, Quezon City (unpublished master's thesis).

JACINTO, Armando S. (1977), An Exploratory Study of Iraya Life and Factors Related to their Popular Participation in Welfare Programs and Services in Oriental Mindoro. University of the Philippines, Manila (unpublished master's thesis).

LAMBERTE, Exaltacion E. (1983), Mangyan Realities: An Integration Study of Contemporary Mangyan Researches (1960-1981), Participatory Upland Management Program, Integrated Research Center Report, De La Salle University, Manila.

LAYKAMM, Magdalena S., SPS (1981), Remedies to Sickness Among the Alangan Mangyans of Oriental Mindoro. Philippine Studies 29:189-216.

LOPEZ, Violeta B. (1976), The Mangyans of Mindoro: An Ethnohistory. University of the Philippines Press, Quezon City.

OTRADEV (1980), An unpublished report.

PAZ, Emerito de la, SVD (1968), A Survey of the Hanunuo Mangyan Culture and Barriers to Change. Unitas 41(1):3-68.

118

POSTMA, Antoon, SVD (1965), The Ambahan of the Hanunuo-Mangyans of Southern Mindoro. Anthropos 60(1-6):358-367.

———— (1969), The Mangyans of Mindoro. (Reprinted from "The Mangyans of Mindoro – Towards Dignity a Better Life").

———— (1981), Treasure of a Minority. Manila, Arnoldus Press, Inc.

SEVILLA, Judy Carol (1983), Indicators of Upland Poverty: A Micro-View in Dimension of Upland Poverty. Integrated Research Center, De La Salle University, Manila.

TWEDDELL, Colin E. (1970), "The Iraya (Mangyan) Language of Mindoro, Philippines: Phonology and Morphology". Unpublished Ph. D. dissertation. University of Washington.

Peter Knecht, S.V.D.

FUNERARY RITES AND THE CONCEPT OF ANCESTORS IN JAPAN

A Challenge to the Christian Churches?

Ancestor worship, or *sosen sūhai,* is one of the favorite topics in Japanese academic circles, but in ordinary speech the term is rarely used, at least in comparison with the importance given to its content. And if the term is used, most people would connect it immediately with Buddhism, because in Japan Buddhism takes care of the dead and the afterlife. And yet, although Buddhism has been instrumental in the formation of an elaborate ritual concerned with the dead and the ancestors, the veneration and respect paid to the ancestors has roots that go beyond Buddhist ritual or doctrine. As has been pointed out again and again, the Japanese attitude toward ancestors partakes of that groundstream of Japan's religious consciousness which gives life to a great number of religious expressions without respect to their particular doctrinal presentation. Ancestor worship is of course also a religious phenomenon, but it is more than that. It is part and parcel of a complex of beliefs, attitudes, obligations, social relations, etc., centered around the ancestors. In order to understand what the ancestors mean in religious terms we also have to keep in mind these other dimensions.[1]

---

[1] Although the term "ancestor" will be explained later in more detail, it should be kept in mind throughout this paper that to speak in general terms about ancestors involves not only a semantic problem, but also questions of local usages and customs, as Smith (1974) has pointed out. In addition, there is the problem of the concept's own history, which has to be seen in tandem with the historical changes that have taken place or are presently occurring within Japanese society. For obvious reasons it is impossible to deal adequately with all of these aspects in a short paper. Consequently, some of the generalizations made here do need more substantiation. However, when I speak of traditional Japanese society, I do not mean to offer an idealized notion of the ancestors for the use of a Christian reinterpretation. Rather, I intend to emphasize that even a new, emerging modern understanding of such a concept has its roots in an older tradition whose influence is still felt. If, then, a Christian uses a traditional terms, but giving it maybe a new meaning, he may occasion misunderstandings. Even if that can be avoided, it will take a considerable length of time before a new interpretation becomes part of the cultural and hence the more unconscious awareness of most Japanese, even

If the attitude towards the ancestors is of such basic importance, then there can hardly be any doubt that the Church in her effort to bring the Gospel to the Japanese cannot afford to disregard it. Here we have one of the core arenas where the encounter of Christian with Japanese ideas has to be negotiated. It is therefore not surprising that the Church, or better the Churches, have been confronted with the problem of how to deal with the ancestors. It is, however, surprising to note that very often the problem is seen merely as one of (Christian) doctrine and rites, and only incidentially as one having some connection with Japanese traditional religious thinking or social relations. I will start by describing the situation in order to show some of the implications of the Japanese concept of ancestors. A discussion of the main features of funerary rites will provide a reasonably "thick description," to use Geertz's term, which will give us, if not exactly a definition, a feeling of what the ancestors are. After laying this groundwork, I will then proceed to delineate some of the practical problems the Church has to face.

A Consideration of Christian Attitudes

The last persecution of *Kirishitan*[2] in Nagasaki was triggered by their refusal to have their dead buried by the priest of the Buddhist temple and by an open statement of their faith in the Lord of Heaven. This fact is quite intriguing if we take into consideration that in more than two hundred years of persecution the *Kirishitan* had developed means of avoiding open conflict with the authorities as much as possible. If pressed to renounce their faith they would do so outwardly, but not in their heart. And afterwards they would

Christians. Before such a goal is attained, if it can ever be reached in a definitive manner, the Christian message itself will go through a period of trial and error until a form is found which integrates with the receiving (and thus to some extent transformed) culture.

[2] *Kirishitan* are the successors of the Christians baptized by the first missionaries after the arrival of Francis Xavier. They practiced their faith secretly during the persecution of the Shogunate until their presence was discovered in 1865 by the French missionary Bernard-Thadée Petitjean. The majority has been reintegrated into the Catholic Church. Others joined other religions. Some remained in hiding until very recently. They are called *kakure kirishitan*, the "hidden Christians".

recite the prayer of *konchirisan* (port. *contrição*), or contrition, in the secrecy of their houses in order to ask God for forgiveness for what they could not avoid without endangering their lives (Kataoka 1979: 203-207).

Only two years after they had come into contact with the newly arrived French missionaries these same people decided that they had to witness to their faith without fear in the face of authority, with the result that several thousand were deported in 1867. This uncompromising standpoint of the *Kirishitan* is referred to and compared explicitly with the present attitude of the Catholic Church by Morioka Kiyomi, a Japanese Christian sociologist of religion. He says: "When we compare this with the present affirmative stance of the Catholic Church towards the performance of the last rites by the temple priest, we find as great a difference as that between heaven and earth" (Morioka 1984: 85). It seems to me that Morioka's sympathy with an uncompromising standpoint towards other religions reflects the opinion of a good number of Christians who think that the two worlds, the Christian and the non-Christian, should be kept strictly apart from each other in any event. Christian faith cannot make a compromise with something non-Christian.

Since the Second Vatican Council the Catholic Church has been making efforts towards serious understanding and appreciation of other peoples' religious feelings and experiences. As a matter of fact, the text to which Morioka refers in order to show the difference between present Catholic practice and that of the *Kirishitan*, is a witness to this new attitude. It is found in a booklet of guidelines for Catholics in dealing with questions arising from veneration of ancestors. I quote the passage:

> "Question 14: I am the successor of the household [*ie*], but since my ancestors and parents were Buddhists, in consideration of my brothers and sisters and other relatives I need to have a Buddhist priest perform the funeral. Would that be allowed?
> Answer: Of course, it is allowed. It goes against the virtue of charity to disregard other people's religion just because oneself is a Catholic. This is a point that always has to be kept in mind" (Christiaens 1980: 21-22; Morioka 1984: 85, n. 15).[3]

---

[3] After Morioka's book was published, the Episcopal Commission for Non-Christians after long deliberation issued official guidelines which make

125

This text is quite noteworthy for its straightforwardness. However, it seems to me that the problem is approached simply through the question of whether a particular ritual can be held by a Christian or not. In the context of Morioka's argument the further question seems to be implied of whether Christians could hold similar rites. But the whole complex of the ancestors encompasses much more than questions of using particular rites, at least if the Church wants to think seriously about the possibility of a Christian form of ancestor worship. This aspect has been brought out by the reactions against the first announcement in the *Katorikku Shinbun* (= *Catholic Weekly*) in February 1983 that the Church is preparing a document on Catholic "ancestor worship".[4] Before I consider the meaning of some of these reactions in their context I have to explain the context, i.e. what the ancestors are and what their role is.

THE JAPANESE CONCEPT OF THE ANCESTORS

Traditionally speaking, it is of primary importance to a Japanese to belong to a "place", (in Japanese *ba*) or a "frame" (*waku*). This frame provides protection and security and demands allegiance and loyalty in return. It is therefore a mutual relationship

---

extensive use of Fr. Christiaens' booklet. In this new edition the passage just quoted is question 11. Although the wording has basically been preserved, the new text further specifies the non-Christian status of the parent or brother/sister. The answer is the same, except for the first sentence where the "of course" has been dropped and the rest of the sentence is expressed in a more cautious form, at the end stating, "It would be allowed". This may look as if it were merely a pecularity of the Japanese language, which often uses indirect forms to soften the impact of such statements. But I feel that the authors had in mind those who might have a problem with a straightforward answer in a question touching not only on cold facts, but which is also laden with deep feelings and convictions.

[4] This is a direct translation of the term which appeared in the weekly. Christiaens prefers, however, to use the term, "ancestor veneration", to avoid the word "worship", arguing that worship is due only to God. Others have proposed the term "ancestral rites", claiming that it would include the idea of having the rites performed "for the benefit of the dead". I shall use "ancestor worship" as it has been used by anthropologists to describe a complex which includes religious as well as social aspects (Berentsen 1983: 3-4; Swyngedouw 1983: 364).

126

which is often expressed as "a bestowal of a favor" and "a returning of a favor". In traditional society one of the classic *loci* for such a relationship is the household, the *ie*.[5] The *ie* is a domestic unit that includes not only those living in the house at a given time, but also extends to the members of past and future generations. Once created, this unit extends ideally into countless generations, providing the primary focus for a person's allegiance and his/her sense of belonging. An *ie* has, therefore, living as well as dead members. In a way the past generations represent the ideal form of an *ie* because their existence is beyond the ordinary vicissitudes of daily life. In reality, however, there is a threat to the very existence of the *ie,* that is, the possibility of its lapsing altogether, if it should happen that the bearer of a line dies without offspring.[6] It is, therefore, the supreme obligation of the head of a household to provide a successor and therewith the guarantee of a future. This is necessary, because the ancestors depend on the services given them by their offspring. In return they guarantee the *ie*'s well-being. Here we have the basics of ancestor worship. Many consider this kind of care for the dead to be the dominant groundstream of Japanese religion as such, conditioning all other religious expression. It has its distinct features that make it into a "religion of the household", in the strict sense of a rather limited social group, and not into the religion of a whole people (Ooms 1967). Robert Smith has formulated this recently, saying that ancestor worship is so much centered on one family or household that "as a consequence, what is proper practice may usefully be defined as what one's household has always done" (Smith 1984; 100). It is therefore a very

---

[5] *Ie* can mean the house as well as the people living in it. In this paper the term is used to include both — the locality and the inhabitants. I shall use this word to underline the aspect of continuity the Japanese term implies. In the cities and under modern employment conditions the family is undergoing a number of significant changes. Nevertheless, certain aspects of the idea of the *ie* are being made use of in other organizations, such as schools or companies. "Traditional" means, therefore, not only that part of the society which still strongly keeps the old customs but also includes those where new forms are molded in analogy to older ones.

[6] Concern about such a possibility could be felt clearly when people learned that I was single in spite of being the only son in our family. They were relived when they heard that a younger sister of mine had *de facto* become the successor. See also note no. 9.

constricted and "land-locked" religion. However, for the members of an *ie* it is imbued with a high degree of intimacy and a consciousness of mutual dependence between the living and the dead.

When pressed for an answer about the whereabouts of the ancestors or the departed, people might say that they have "gone to heaven". But the ordinary behavior of the same people tells quite a different story. For the first fifty days after a person's death it is said that the spirit still lingers on around the house where the deceased had spent his life. A woman whose husband had died suddenly in his sleep told me once that every night until the forty-ninth day she felt how he would creep in under her quilt. Something like this is not at all an unusual story. But once this period is over the departed is said to have gone away. From that time on he can be addressed together with those who had passed away earlier without much formality at the *butsudan,* the Buddhist ancestral altar in the house where the ancestral tablets are kept. Or he may be visited at or invited from the grave. The departed, although living in another world, continue to be intimately related to the living members of the *ie.*[7] They are esteemed as those who provided once for those who are now living, and so they are thought of as being still closely concerned with the well-being of the *ie* and its protection (Smith 1974: 127). On the other hand, they depend on the care of the living for their own comfort. In a traditional household the ancestors are offered food and drink in the same way as the members of the family. The family will eat only after the ancestors have received their portion. On certain days they are especially welcomed into the house for a short period. In any case, they are thought of as being close and taking a keen interest in the events of the household.

---

[7] In a recent opinion poll 59% of those interviewed said that they strongly felt close to the ancestors. Broken down into age groups the numbers reveal that the feeling of closeness increases with advancing age. On the other hand old people believe less in the existence of a "soul", *reikon,* after death. The belief in the existence of *hotoke* increased, however, with an increase in age. *Hotoke* is the common term for a recently deceased person. It is possible that older people did not understand the term "soul" very well, an experience I had repeatedly during my field work, but the poll is not clear about this (NHK 1984: 11: 44-46).

However, not all of the departed are of the same status from the moment of their death. Those who died recently are considered to be still in need of certain ritual assistance in order to attain full ancestorhood. Their memory is still alive among the living. They are often addressed as *hotoke,* buddha.[8] The departed in this state are still involved in an ongoing process of development towards ancestorhood. Ancestors in the full sense of the word, on the other hand, are in a state of serenity that knows no further development, at least for most of them. They are just remembered as "the ancestors", *sorei,* without particular names or any other characteristics. Their identity has been absorbed into a general category (Plath 1964: 302-303).

FUNERARY RITES: AN OUTLINE

There is no other ritual complex that expresses the relationship between the living and the dead, i.e., the ancestors, more emphatically than the funerary rites. In the following I will take up some of their main features, but I will concentrate mainly on the concept of ancestors and its social implications, because, as we have seen already, the two cannot be separated from each other.

Death is the first step on the road to ancestorhood and marks a radical change, but it does not separate the departed completely from the *ie.* The change that has occurred finds vivid expression in a number of symbolic actions representing a clear inversion of everyday life. Soon after the person has expired, the body is washed and dressed, but the dress has to be sewn by as many women as possible and care is taken that it looks carelessly put together and that the ends of the pieces of cloth which are used do not fit neatly together. The garment is then put on the body in such a way that it closes with that side on top that would be underneath on a living person. The body is then bedded into quilts like a sleeping person, but its head is turned towards north, a direction that is often

---

[8] *Hotoke* can be a term designating a corpse. Further, it includes the Japanese idea that a person of his death becomes a buddha, a fact which is given concrete expression by the posthumous name which is inscribed on the ancestral tablet and the tomb stone. See also note 5.

painstakingly avoided when people go to sleep. Behind the pillow there is a small altar with some offerings but also a folding screen which has been put up upside down.

The night before the burial a short ceremony is held by the priest, and the relatives of the deceased stay up late, exchanging memories about the dead. This is in fact the last time when the whole family and only the family is together with its deceased member. On the day of the burial the Buddhist priest comes again and prepares first two wooden tablets by inscribing them with the posthumous name of the departed. One of them will be taken by the funeral procession to the cemetery, the other will remain in the house until the forty-ninth day after death, when it too may be brought to the grave to be left to decay. Besides a wooden *tōba*, the token of a stupa, the priest inscribes another board with the names of seven Buddhas. This is brought to the grave on the seventh day after death has occurred and it designates the seven worlds of Buddhas the departed has to go through during the first forty-nine days after death. During that period, every week on the memorial day somebody, possibly the head of the family, visits the grave. With each elapsing week the deceased is thought to become increasingly purified until on the forty-ninth day, he/she loses any material connection with the place where he/she lived. In the house a special kind of altar has been built over the coffin. After the burial the main parts of the altar are kept until the hundredth day, when the immediate period of the funeral finally ends. After that the new tablet is put into the ordinary ancestor shelf.

A year after the day of death a first anniversary service is held. Similar celebrations will be held after 3, 7, 13, 17, 23, 27 and finally after 33 years. Because these celebrations involve quite a large financial expense, not everybody will be able to hold all of them, but the last, called *tomurai-age*, "the lifting of memorials", usually receives special attention. It marks the moment when the departed has finally become an ancestor in the full sense and thus has definitely joined the group of an *ie*'s forebears. After that the tablet is deposited in the temple or on the grave, and so even this last piece of individual identity is lost.

At this point, whereas the person has disintegrated as an individual, he/she has become fully integrated into the larger entity of the *ie* where he/she is in close communion with the living.

130

Notwithstanding the radical change which has occurred in the individual, the ancestor or the collectivity of ancestors is an essential part of the *ie* and is even the source of its well-being. The ancestors are in a very real sense seen as the protectors of the household (Komatsu and Tatematsu 1984: 176). This finds a special expression when some of the ancestors merge with the agricultural deities who bestow material daily livelihood upon the living.

Theoretically, every human being could become an ancestral spirit. Social conditions, however, determine whether a particular person will in fact become an ancestor or not. As Smith's study on ancestral tablets has shown, people do not always do what they say they do. And so it happens that in the ancestors's shelf they include individuals who, according to theory, would have no place there, because they do not fulfill the social condition of belonging to the *ie*. But in spite of this we can say that membership, even membership of a special kind, in the *ie* is the precondition for becoming an ancestor one day. To be a member one has to be born or adopted into the *ie*, but in order to eventually become an ancestor., one has further to have a successor. Therefore, to marry can be seen as the basic condition or even as the first and necessary step on the way to final ancestorhood (Ooms 1967: 291).[9]

Any death affects not only the person who has died, but also the survivors. Speaking from my own field experience in a rural area of Northern Japan, I would like to distinguish three groups of persons who are affected each in a different way by the death of a villager.[10] The first and central group is, of course, the family of the departed and its relatives. The family is really the nucleus and center of the rites, at least of most of them, but it plays a rather passive role especially in the early stages of the funerary process. It appears to be grouped with the departed in a kind of polluting relationship which excludes the family members from rituals for the *kami* and from certain community activities where a celebration for the

---

[9] This does not mean that the successor has to be an offspring of the household head's marriage. Adoption was, and still is, used as a convenient means to make up for the absence of natural or desired offspring. See also note 4.

[10] The same would apply to other rural areas. In the cities some of the community's duties have been taken over by professional undertakers and at times by the deceased's employer.

kami[11] would be involved. Contact with them is also polluting for others, particularly through the means of shared fire. The family shares the food with its dead member, but others avoid eating something that has been cooked on the same fire as that of the family.

When the funeral procession is formed after the last rites in the house, for the first time the core group, the family, emerges from seclusion before the eyes of the outside world. At this moment it demonstrates the significant changes that have occurred in the alignment of its members by their relative position in the procession. But at the same time it also demonstrates the continuing unity of the *ie*. The members of the family form the center of the procession around the coffin. The head or the new head of the *ie* is the one to carry the tablet of the deceased, which can be seen as the focal point where the worlds of the ancestors and of the living meet. This clearly underscores the new composition of the *ie*, together with its continuity.

Continuity is not only demonstrated, it is also truly guaranteed by new births, and so the women of the family walk behind the coffin holding on to a long piece of white cloth which is attached to the coffin. It's name, "the rope of life", is a clear reference to the women as the bearers of life which they pass on in the line of the person who just has died. This is further underlined by what happens to this cloth once the party has arrived at the temple or the cemetery. Whereas nothing of all the other things that are used at the grave may be brought back into the house, this white "rope of life" can be claimed by a woman to take home. She will wrap it around her womb during the last weeks of pregnancy because it is believed that it will help to ensure a safe delivery.

Once the burial is over, the family is left alone and assumes its responsibility for the departed and for the grave. Before this, two other groups play a very important and prominent role: the close neighbors and the hamlet community. Both groups operate on a principle of reciprocity, because it is understood that any help

---

[11] The term *kami* is used for a variety of superhuman beings in Japanese religious tradition, but here it stands mainly for the Japanese deities as being distinct from Buddhas or from the Christian God. A problem arises because the term is used for God in Christian language. In this paper it is used only for Japanese deities.

extended will be returned when the occasion arises. In fact, all the other visitors at the funeral who just pay their respects and give a contribution to be used for the needs of the bereaved family are treated according to this same principle. They all receive a small token present in return and their names and contributions are carefully recorded on a list which will be kept and referred to when there is need to make an appropriate contribution in return.

The closer of the two groups are the neighbors who are something like an extension of the household. There is a Japanese expression that is quite often quoted by villagers and says "Three houses in front and one on each side". It means that no matter whether good or bad fortune strikes a house, these neighbors will also be affected by it. People in this group feel a specially strong obligation to go and extend a helping hand to each other. Together with the more distant relatives or the in-laws of the bereaved family they take care of the affairs in the house such as attending to guests, preparing and serving meals, etc.

The last group is taken from the hamlet. It is involved in a more formally established manner, because it is a funerary association that has the responsibility of organizing the funeral as such. They see to it that the relatives are duly informed about the death and the time of the funeral, that the grave is prepared and the procession organized. They also carry the coffin and a number of items that go with any funeral procession. It is a voluntary group. but in a small hamlet every household is represented and can therefore count on its assistance. The contribution of both groups to the funeral is fulfilled with the end of the funeral proper, but often the neighbors make regular visits to the new grave on the weekly memorial days until the forty-ninth day.

Here we witness a network of mutual cooperation which is active in a double sense. First it emphasizes the unity and continuity of the *ie* group in spite of a momentary crisis. Second it reaffirms the *ie*'s role as part of a lateral, and not too formal, organization, the hamlet, which itself shows characteristics similar to those of the *ie*, although on a different level. This means that the hamlet, too, is a group that extends through time and is formed by a shared locality. In contrast to the *ie*, the hamlet is not organized by a single line, but, like the *ie*, it operates, at least ideally speaking, through the loyal mutual cooperation of the different *ie* groups.

All the rites mentioned so far can be performed only once for any particular individual. There are, however, further rites which recur regularly and after certain fixed periods. It is convenient to distinguish two types: one that is repeated every year, and one that is performed only once in several years. The first type involves mainly the immediate family and those born from the current head. These are the celebrations of *higan,* the spring and autumn equinox, and of *bon,* the mid-summer festival of the dead. Visits to the graves and special attention given to the ancestral altar are the main features of these celebrations. The regular memorials are of the second type. Such celebrations have a more formal character and bring together quite a large group of relatives. These ceremonies involve a rite performed by the priest at the ancestral altar, then a visit to the grave and a common meal. The official (or theological) purpose of this ceremony is to turn over the merits of the rites to the dead to help him to advance further on the road to full ancestorhood. However, the participants do not always appear to have a clear idea about this religious aspect. They certainly want to renew their closeness to a particular departed person and through the departed also to their relatives whom they otherwise almost might forget, and I was told repeatedly that the meaning of these celebrations, after all, is to bring together the offspring of the one who is remembered. They are, therefore, reunions of more or less distant relatives, the degree of distance depending on how far the departed has advanced toward the last stages of the process. Reunions for a person who has died long ago tend to become increasingly formal, and once the last memorial has been held connections among distant relatives of that ancestor's generation may easily be allowed to fall into oblivion. The moment the deceased becomes a full ancestor, there occurs a double sort of oblivion: the oblivion of the ancestor's own individuality, and the oblivion of the relatives who forget to trace their line to him. After a time during which his offspring and those of his siblings form a larger group of relatives expanding beyond the single *ie,* the departed finally comes back, so to speak, to where everything started at birth, *viz.,* the *ie.* As long as personal traits are remembered, they provide enough reason to hold together quite a large group of individuals, but the degree of intimacy binding the group together decreases with the increase in distance from the remembered person.

Taking all of this into consideration, we can conclude that the ancestors in Japan are more than just a concept in the minds of people. They take on a new kind of reality in the social group of those living members forming one household in succession to the ancestors. The care of the ancestors therefore involves not only a spiritual or religious attitude, but also demands the fulfillment of social obligations which are strongly felt, even if one changes one's religious convictions or has no particular convictions at all. In this sense ancestor veneration or worship means dedication to the *ie*. Therefore, the successor turned Christian in the short text quoted above is still expected to do what is his duty as a successor to the *ie*. This expectation even finds legal expression when the Japanese Civil Code stipulates that the successor has care of the ancestors and the ritual objects going with this, without making any reference to a particular religious conviction.[12]

THE REACTION OF THE CHURCH TO THE ANCESTORS

How does the Church react to this situation in her efforts to bring the Gospel to the Japanese? Let me start with a quote from a study made by the priest of an urban parish. He asked a hundred parishioners about the day when they would remember their dead. Only two gave All Souls' Day, most of them said it would be *bon* or *higan*. Then he comments on the findings in the following manner: "Of the one hundred Catholics, almost half of them, forty-seven, have Buddhist services and twenty-eight have Catholic services performed and some twenty-five do nothing for their dead. Since one quarter do nothing for their dead, one wonders whether something in Christianity is responsible for the negligence towards the dead in a country where respect for the dead is so much a part of their cultural heritage" (Doerner 1977: 174).

Knowing nothing about the social background of these Catholics it is difficult to assess the author's judgement of

---

[12] The post-War Civil Code did abolish the *ie* organization in the form of the pre-War Family System. Nevertheless, the authors of the Civil Code could not decide, even after long discussions, to do away with the traditional form of inheritance for the ritual items harbored by the household (Takeda 1976: 188-193).

"negligence". On the other hand, his conclusion cannot entirely be dismissed as just too pessimistic or misled. It might in fact be a result of the Church's influence or reflect a presumably Christian standpoint towards non-Christian or also towards Christian dead.

We know that this problem has a long history in the Catholic Church and especially in Asia recalls memories of a difficult period. Personally, I find it quite significant that Japan was instrumental in bringing about a certain opening in the Church's attitude in the so-called Question of Rites. Directly or indirectly the new pronouncements on the question in the thirties of this century were prompted by or related to Japan. Based on a Japanese Government declaration, the Congregation for the Propagation of Faith instructed the Apostolic Delegate in Tokyo that Christians could take part in rites at shrines or in funerals provided that they made it clear that they understand such rites to be only of a civil nature. As one of the reasons for this decision the Congregation refers to an evolution in time and customs which had the result of divesting the rites of their original religious content (Sylloge 1939: 539-540). Permission to participate was given with the understanding that these rites had lost their religious significance. In a second instruction given in 1939 a similar interpretation is expressed again and the obligation of an oath for the priests abrogated (AAS 1940: 24-26). However, the reminder of Benedict XIV's interdiction of 1742 was upheld, including the prohibition to discuss the question. I will return to this problem later. Suffice it for the moment to say that we do not lack examples where formerly religious rites ended up as purely civil ceremonies. On the other hand there is also the danger of reading into unfamiliar concepts or behavior a meaning which is taken to be there just because they happen to have certain similarities with Christian concepts or behavior.[13] Strictly speaking

---

[13] Gernet shows just what kind of difficulties such interpretations can lead to in his fascinating study of Chinese reactions toward the missionary efforts of the early Jesuits. He argues that even a man like Matteo Ricci made the mistake of being too quick in finding parallels between Western (i.e., scholastic) and Chinese philosophical terms. His observations are of particular interest because they are based on an analysis of the reactions of the Chinese literati against the Jesuit missionaries' effort to integrate Christian ideas with Confucian thought (Gernet 1982: 191-223; 263-283). For the situation in Africa Ela has shown that similar difficulties and dangers result from an approach inspired by Western ideas (Ela 1977: 38-43). Their observations are well worth being considered also in a Japanese context.

the documents mentioned are concerned with non-Christian rites and the possibility of Christians taking part in them, but they do not address the possibility of creating similar rites in Christian ritual. Had the documents addressed this latter question, they would have had to take into account the importance which attitudes towards ancestors may also have for Christians.

After Vatican II the problem was felt anew and attempts have been made to help Christians in deciding what to do in particular cases, or to find a Christian expression for remembering the ancestors. Father Christiaens' booklet and the latest publication by the Episcopal Commission for Non-Christian Religions reflect this new attitude. Both documents are composed with a pastoral purpose in mind. They are not meant to be doctrinal declarations (Episcopal Commission 1985: 3). The Commission's document refers to the Mystical Body of Christ as the basis which unites the living and the dead. A Christian's love for his forebears can find expression in prayers for the dead, and the saints may intervene with God for the sake of the faithful, but it is made clear that they do not have any special power by themselves. The document also states explicitly that to remember and venerate the dead does not mean that they are worshipped as God, *kami,* is worshipped.[14] It then goes on to refer to God's intention to save all mankind, which would include also those who in fact did not personally embrace the Christian faith. This last explanation is given in a section about "communion with the ancestors in Japan", and it says that, based on faith in God's saving intention, it is necessary to express one's love towards the ancestors. It is, however, quite noteworthy that the word "ancestor" is used here, whereas it is not used in the first part of the document where the Christian attitude is explained. There the document speaks about "communion with the dead". This, it seems to me, indicates a significant shift of emphasis from a particular

---

[14] Although it can be said that the Christian, or at least a monotheistic, concept of God, is not without influence on the contemporary Shintō interpretation of the characteristics of a *kami,* it should be kept in mind that this term, especially when it is used in connection with the ancestors, may have reverberations in the mind of a Japanese which are not present in the Christian or Western understanding of the concept of God. The text, produced for Catholics, uses the word *kami* which here has to be understood in the Catholic sense of God, but somebody with a feeling for the situation where an ancestor can become a *kami* at times, clearly senses the difficulty. See also note no. 8.

group's ancestors to the community of all the living with all the dead in Christ. A similar idea pervades the rites in the Ritual for Funerals, which centers on the mystery of Christ's death and resurrection in which the Christian shares in virtue of being immersed in Christ through Baptism. Consequently, emphasis is given to Christian hope in the face of death. The Ritual would allow for the use of local customs as long as they do not contradict this spirit of the Gospel. Compared with what I have said about the ancestors, there can be no doubt that all this signifies an important and characteristically Christian new understanding which is fundamentally different from the ordinary Japanese concept of the ancestors and the obligations toward them.

It is, therefore, not surprising that the first announcement in the *Catholic Weekly* about the Episcopal Commission's preparing a document on *sosen sūhai*, "ancestor worship", met with strong reaction from some Christians and some non-Christians alike. For both groups the term "ancestor worship" used by an official group of the Catholic Church was the stumbling block. Christians seem to have understood the term more in the traditional Japanese sense and so they felt that the Church was engaged in abandoning her treasured values. They felt that they were betrayed. They had embraced the Christian faith to get away from all this, and did not understand what the Church was up to. On the other hand, non-Christians saw a different kind of danger. Some feared that such an approach by the Church could be used by those forces who are trying to revive a kind of State Shintō and bring back the pre-War situation with the emperor's line as the ultimate ancestral line of all Japanese.[15] Others, e.g. on the Shintō side, saw it not as an attempt at spiritual rapprochement or as a revision of the essence of Christianity, but rather as "a discussion only about whether one can or cannot 'change qualitatively' the mentality of ancestor veneration itself so as to make it conformable to the essence of

---

[15] This concern is shared by many Protestant Christians as well. I think that it cannot be resolved just by relying on an official declaration of the Government or on the expected impact of a new doctrinal interpretation. In Japan as well as China, although in somewhat different ways, there exists a long tradition of closely linked political and religious thought (cf. Gernet 1982: 143-153). To ignore other possible aspects of a term just because one is concerned only with one aspect, i.e., the religious aspect, would seem to be quite naive.

Christianity" (Swyngedouw 1983: 362). They felt that a treasured concept was being used as a cover to introduce silently a new meaning. I do not think that they were entirely mistaken in their assumption, because I see the pronouncement as an instance of an attitude employing a "transformation model" for its approach to the problem (Tracy 1977: 97). From these reactions it is evident that the Church's position is not without problems, but I feel that it is the only attitude allowing for creative flexibility, on condition that the implications of such a transformation are reckoned with. We have to see that cultural meanings are involved here, which, although quite stable, are not permanently fixed. They can undergo changes, as a result of changes in the environment or of the impact of a new ideology, philosophy or religion. It is, however, important to keep in mind that such a rearrangement of meanings and interpretations is rarely a completely one-way affair, for it may affect all partners, although in different degrees. As for Christian ideas, one has to reckon with the fact, or at least the possibility, that ideas of the receiving partner influence to some degree the expression and formulation of Christian teachings.

This aspect has been addressed by Nishiyama in a study about the effects of indigenization on the believers' faith in a largely Christian village. Focussing on the importance of an ancestral cult and the presence or absence of an ancestral altar in Christian families, he finds that 38.5% of the Christians remember their dead with a feeling of respect, but do not pray to them as to *kami* or buddhas for divine protection. He concludes that the Christians "succeeded to a fairly high degree in extricating themselves from the traditional ancestral cult" (Nishiyama 1985: 52), and is inclined to see it as an instance of change in the ancestral cult. These Christians did not have an ancestral altar. However, he also found that 26.3% of the Christians confronted the ancestors with a "feeling of praying to the *kami* or the buddhas for protection" (Nishiyama 1985: 53). Since these were those Christians who possessed an ancestral altar, he interprets their attitude as a "substantive change in the Christianity of this community" caused by the ancestral cult. It might be questioned whether such a conclusion can be legitimately reached by sociological methods, but the answers of the villagers cannot be brushed off as completely irrelevant. Their case shows, at least in adumbrations, that a process of transformation works in two directions.

CONCLUSION

If the Church wants to give directions within such a framework, they can be given only when a serious effort is made to understand what the ancestors are, not only in religious but also in social terms. For such a purpose, it seems to me, it is vital that the Church trust her faithful and enlist their help. I do not mean to say that responsibility can simply be tossed on other shoulders, but I do think that openness means trust in the responsible actions of those who embrace the faith, that is, the Japanese Christians. In fact, the Roman documents I have mentioned invariably consider it necessary to have the Christians come to their own responsible decisions. As Offner concludes his contribution to a recent discussion on ancestor worship, "while Western Christians may give their sympathetic counsel regarding these domestic memorial rites as outsiders, it is finally the Japanese Christians themselves who must determine whether or not their motivations and actions are in keeping with or in violation of scriptural truth and the spirit of Christ" (Offner 1983: 34). No doubt, this involves also time, considerable time. I feel that if the Church is looking for fast results in a process involving broad cultural changes, she is forgetting her own (European) history.

As we have seen, there are many more things involved in ancestor worship than just problems of doctrine and its expression in a particular rite. As Morioka has observed very succinctly, to remember the ancestors constitutes a stream of thought that flows through all Japanese from of old. It is the religious foundation for the common people (Ogawa *et al.* 1981: 23). In other words, it is the main stream of folk religion, which does not offer a system of rationally organized ideas about the ancestors, but a satisfying solution about the problem of life and death, supported by beliefs and customs which respond to a deep-seated longing of the people. Thus, it does not come as a surprise any more when one reads that modernization in Japan had consequences mainly on a highly intellectual level but did not reach the deeper consciousness of the people, which in turn supports the traditional community (Ogawa *et al.* 1981: 25). I think that this "deeper consciousness" is the area where the principle of reciprocity mentioned above comes into play. Of course, the new situations in the cities may eventually bring about changes in the composition of families and ultimately in the form of ancestor worship. The idea of the household as a continuing entity through time may indeed lose its importance and ancestor worship may decline insofar as it is connected with the *ie*. The question, however, is whether the ancestors are essentially linked to the structure of the *ie* and therefore would necessarily have to share its fate. The feeling of closeness to the ancestors, supported by the conviction that they grant protection and that therefore one has to be loyal to them, lies deeper than any particular social form which may provide the frame within which those feelings come into play. I think that Japanese ancestor worship is primarily rooted in the "ethos" of Japanese culture, which is characterized by reciprocity and loyalty, attitudes that find expression in relationships of receiving and returning favors. It is quite conceivable that this ethos of Japanese culture is not fatefully connected with the existence or non-existence of an *ie*-organization in the narrow sense of this word. Therefore, even if the family ended up as a unit of people who may choose freely for which of their forebears they may wish to care, it could still be an expression of that obligation which the living feel towards some of the departed from whom they have received special favors. For that reason I think that a change in the organization of the family does not have to bring with it a change in the basic attitude towards the ancestors and consequently would not necessitate the disappearance of ancestor worship. As a consequence it remains a feature of Japanese culture challenging the Church beyond merely ritual adaptation.

PETER KNECHT, S.V.D.

REFERENCES CITED

AAS (1940), *Acta Apostolicae Sedis, Commentarium Officiale*. Vol. XXXII, Roma.

BERENTSEN, Jan-Martin (1983), The Ancestral Rites in Missiological Perspective. *Japanese Religions,* vol. 13, no. 1: 2-27.

CHRISTIAENS, Michel (1980), *Katorikku no senzo sūkei* (Catholic Ancestor Veneration). Tokyo. (In Japanese).

DOERNER, David L. (1977), Comparative Analysis of Life after Death in Folk Shinto and Christianity. *Japanese Journal of Religious Studies,* vol. 4: 151-18; 2.

ELA, Jean-Marc (1977), Ancestors and Christian Faith: An African Problem, *Concilium* 102: 34-50.

Episcopal Commission for Non-Christian Religions (1985), *Sosen to shisha ni tsuite no katorikku shinja no tebiki* (A Guide for Catholics Concerning the Ancestors and the Dead). Tokyo. (In Japanese).

GERNET, Jacques (1982), *Chine et christianisme. Action et réaction.* Paris: Gallimard.

KATAOKA Yakichi (1979), *Fumie — kinkyō no rekishi (Fumie —* A History of the Ban on Religion) Tokyo. (In Japanese).

KOMATSU Kazuhiko, TATEMATSU Kazuhira (1984), *Takai wo wāpu suru. Minzokushakai kōgi* (Spain the Other World) Tokyo. (In Japanese).

MORIOKA Kiyomi (1984), *Ie no henbō to senzo no matsuri* (Transformation of the *ie* and the Celebrations for the Ancestors). Tokyo. (In Japanese).

NHK (Japanese Broadcasting Company) (1984), *Nihonjin no shūkyō ishiki* (The Religious Consciousness of the Japanese). Tokyo. (In Japanese).

NISHIYAMA Shigeru (1985), Indigenization and Transformation of Christianity in a Japanese Rural Community. *Japanese Journal of Religious Studies,* vol. 12: 17-61.

OFFNER, Clark (1983), A Cloud of Witnesses. *Japanese Religions,* vol. 13, no. 1: 28-34.

OGAWA Keiji *et al.* (1981), Gendai shūkyō e no shikaku (A Look at Modern Religion). *Juristo sōgō tokushū* no. 21: 19-34. (In Japanese).

OOMS, Herman (1967), The Religion of the Household. A Case Study of Ancestor Worship in Japan. *Contemporary Religions in Japan,* vol. 8: 201-333.

PLATH, David (1964), Where the Family of God is the Family. *American Anthropologist* 66: 300-317.

SMITH, Robert J. (1974), *Ancestor Worship in Contemporary Japan.* Stanford.

—— (1984), Japanese Religious Attitudes from the Standpoint of the Comparative Study of Civilizations. *Senri Ethnological Studies* no. 16: 99-104.

SWYNGEDOUW, Jan (1983), In Search of a Church with a Japanese Face (5): The Problem of Ancestor Veneration. *The Japan Missionary Bulletin,* vol. 37: 360-366.

Sylloge (1939), *Sylloge.* Praecipuorum documentarum recentium Summorum Pontificum et S. Congregationis de Propaganda Fide necnon aliarum SS. Congregationum Romanarum. Ad usum missionariorum. Roma.

TAHARA Yukio (1985), "Seisho no genten" Katorikku no shinhōshin (The Bible as Basis, the New Catholic Policy). *Mainichi Shinbun, yūkan,* 5th March, p. 4.

TAKEDA Chōshū (1976), *Nihonjin no ie to shūkyō (Ie* and the Religion of the Japanese). Tokyo. (In Japanese).

TRACY, David (1977), Ethnic Pluralism and Systematic Theology. *Concilium* 101: 91-99.

Joseph Dinh Duc Dao

INCULTURATION OF THE PRAYER-LIFE
OF THE CHURCH IN ASIA:
THE CASE OF ZEN MEDITATION

Asia is a continent vast in both land and population: 2,674,879,000 inhabitants to a surface of 44,000,000 km². [1] In ecclesiastical geography, Asia is sub-divided into 4 regions: *South-West Asia* which is commonly known as the Middle East; *South Asia* which is composed of Afghanistan, Bangladesh, India, Pakistan and Sri Lanka: *East Asia* which is composed of mainland China, China Taiwan, Hong Kong, Japan, Korea, Macao, Mongolia, etc.; *South-East Asia* which is composed of Burma, Indonesia, the Khmer Republic, Laos, Malaysia, the Philippines, Singapore, Thailand and Vietnam. [2]

A look into the sub-divisions gives us a picture of Asia which shows not only a vast continent, but one which is also very much diversified in race, language, custom, culture, religious tradition, etc., so that one may say that Asia is more a conventional concept than a reality. Therefore, it seems impossible to make a thorough report and reflection on the efforts toward inculturation in Asia as a whole.

As for prayer: from the point of view of the Christian life, prayer is a general term which indicates all forms of worship private prayer, community prayer, contemplative prayer, liturgical prayer, etc. In this context, a reflection on the inculturation of prayer should cover all the fields of theology, mysticism, symbols, rites, etc. When we look at this from the point of view of the non-Christian religions, we find that Asia is very rich in religious traditions: Islamic, Hindu, Buddhist, Taoist, with their various rich and numerous prayer experiences. There are, in addition, numerous local religious traditions which also have their own prayer expressions.

Confronted with this vast field of the inculturation of the prayer-life of the Church in Asia, this paper will limit itself to the

---

[1] Cf. AIMIS, no. 366, 1 agosto 1983; cf. *Grand Larousse Encyclopedia,* Tome 3e, 1960, p. 447.

[2] Cf. Sacra Congregazione per l'Evangelizzazione dei Popoli, *Guide delle Missioni Cattoliche 1975,* 1975, p. 361-366; 543-611.

Buddhist tradition, and to the contemplative form of prayer. More precisely, this paper will examine only those efforts which seek to integrate in the Christian prayer-life the form of prayer which is called *Zen* in Japanese, *Ch'an* in Chinese, *Thiên* in Vietnamese. Geographically, this paper refers to the countries which take part in the FABC,[3] or more precisely, to those countries such as China, Japan, Thailand, Indonesia, India, the Philippines and Vietnam where Zen influences can be clearly felt. Thus, all through the paper I would like to keep present these necessary restrictions.

I. NECESSITY OF INCULTURATION: CONSCIOUSNESS OF THE CHURCH IN ASIA

The history of the inculturation of the Gospel in Asia will mark the 16th and 17th century as its decisive moment, if not as its starting point. In fact, these were the centuries of Fr. Matteo Ricci (1550-1610), missionary of China; Fr. Roberto de Nobili (1577-1656), missionary of India, and Fr. Alexandre de Rhodes (1591-1660), missionary of Vietnam, who tried successfully to integrate the Gospel with the local cultures.

However, in this period, the need of inculturation was far from being a general conviction in the Church in Asia. It tended to be limited to the efforts of these great missionaries and their companions. Only gradually has the need of inculturating the Gospel in Asian life and cultures gained ground in the mind of Asian Christians, clearing away resistance and suspicion. Thus, nowadays, inculturation can be considered to be a general conviction in the churches of Asia, and it was definitively accepted by the FABC in its Plenary Assemblies in 1974 and 1978.

In the general context of inculturation, the Plenary Assembly of the FABC in 1974 declared that "to preach the Gospel in Asia today we must make the message and life of Christ truly incarnate in the minds and lives of our peoples. The primary focus of our task

---

[3] FABC = Federation of the Asian Bishops' Conferences. At present, it has 14 full members (Bangladesh, Burma, China Taiwan, India, Indonesia, Japan, Korea, Laos-Khmer Republic, Malaysia-Singapore, the Philippines, Pakistan, Sri Lanka, Thailand, Vietnam), and 2 associates (Hong Kong and Macao).

of evangelization then, at this time in our history, is the building up of a truly local church .... The local church is a church incarnate in a people, a church in continuous, humble and loving dialogue with the living traditions, the cultures, the religions — in brief, with all the life realities of the people in whose midst it has sunk its roots deeply and whose history and life it gladly makes its own. It seeks to share in whatever truly belongs to that people: its meanings and its values, its aspirations, its thoughts and its language, its songs and its artistry. Even its fralities and failings it assumes, so that they too may be healed. For so did God's Son assume the totality of our fallen human condition (save only for sin) so that he might make it truly his own, and redeem it in his paschal mystery".[4]

The inculturation of prayer-life was specifically studied during the Plenary Assembly of the FABC in 1978. On this occasion, it was acknowledged that "more than ever there is need of integrating our Christian prayer into everyday life.... In keeping with the economy of the Incarnation, which is the law of the Church's life and mission, the prayer-life of our local churches should 'take over the riches of our nations, which have been given to Christ as an inheritance' (AG 22; cf. AG 11; LG 13-17; FABC I, par. 9-12, 20-21). Important above all, in our present context, are those ways of prayer which have been developed by the native genius of our peoples and have played a vital and honored role in shaping the traditions of our lands. We are daily more convinced that the Spirit is leading us in our time, not to some dubious syncretism (which we all rightly reject), but to an integration — profound and organic in character — of all that is best in our Christian heritage. Thus is a fuller catholicity made possible in this age of the Church.... In the past, the integration of some of these elements has sometimes been the object of hesitancy and suspicion. We believe that with deeper study and understanding, with prudent discernment on our part and proper catechesis of our Christian people, these many indigenous riches will at last find a natural place in the prayer of our churches in Asia and will greatly enrich the prayer-life of the Church throughout the world".[5]

---

[4] Statement of the First Plenary Assembly of the FABC, Taipei, 27th April, 1974, nn. 9, 12 in: *FABC Papers*, n° 28, p. 16.
[5] Final Statement of the Second Plenary Assembly of the FABC, Calcutta, 25th November, 1978, nn. 27, 30-31, 33 in: *FABC Papers*, n° 13, p. 19-20.

Along with these declarations, one should not forget the numerous studies on this subject done by theologians in these recent years.[6] All these clearly manifest the mind of the Churches of Asia on inculturation.

II. EXPERIENCES OF THE INCULTURATION OF PRAYERLIFE

The declarations of the Plenary Assemblies of the FABC approve and encourage the experiments in the inculturation of prayer-life which have been carried on for some time in various local churches in Asia. In these last years, one can witness a growing desire among Asian Catholics to live out their faith and to pray in ways that belong to their own indigenous cultures. Thus, one sees quite a number of priests, religious brothers and sisters, and lay Catholics "sitting" quietly. Sometimes they just sit silently, sometimes they use some words like a variation of the "Jesus prayer" in the form of a Zen "koan". Others sit at the feet of a Buddhist master, and under his direction, they practise Zen as it is and go through the Zen "koan", considering these forms of meditation an authentic Christian prayer.

Although all these efforts toward inculturating Zen in Christian prayer-life are similar in desire and spirit, they are different in approach. Four approaches can be identified: some practise Zen as a *preparation* for prayer; others practise Zen as a *way of dialogue with Buddhists*; others look on Zen as a *form of Christian prayer*; others still use the *Zen form adapting it* to the Christian faith.[7]

---

[6] DIVARKAR P.R., "Reflection on the problem of inculturation", in: *FABC Papers*, n° 7, p. 1-8; *id., "Evangelii Nuntiandi* and the problem of inculturation", in: *Teaching All Nations*, 15 (1978), 226-232; BULATAO J., REILLY J., WILCKEN J., CLAVER F.F., *Inculturating Christianity in East Asia*, in: *FABC Papers*, n° 7, p. 18-35; RATNA BAMRUNGTRAKUL R., *Inculturation and mission*, in: *Omnis Terra*, 17 (1983), 319-323; HARDAWIRYANA R., *The growing Church: Amid various Religious and Cultural Traditions and contemporary Ideologies*, in: *FABC Papers*, n° 14, etc. (see Bibliography below).

[7] Fr. William JOHNSTON sees rather three different approaches: Zen as a preparation for Christian prayer; Zen as a way of dialogue with Buddhists, and Zen as a form of Christian prayer, cf. William JOHNSTON, *Zen – The present situation*, in: *EAPR*, 20 (1983), 340.

1. *Zen as a preparation for Christian prayer*

Those who take Zen as a preparation for prayer would learn to sit quietly in the lotus posture, to breathe from the abdomen, to still their heart and to concentrate their mind. When they have reached the interior silence, they do their prayer as they have always done. It is quite clear that in this approach, Zen is taken as a technique of concentration and interiority, but, strictly speaking, they are not praying.

From the theological point of view, this approach does not cause problems. But can we consider it inculturation? The answer depends very much on the vision which one has of inculturation. The phenomenon of inculturation is very complex, and can be very different according to the situations of life. Therefore, the vision of inculturation can also be different in different persons. I would like to take two descriptions of inculturation from which we may formulate an answer for the problem in question.

According to the Second Plenary Assembly of the FABC in 1978, inculturation is not some dubious syncretism, but an integration, profound and organic in character, of all that is best in the traditional ways of prayer and worship into the treasury of the Christian heritage.[8]

The second description is taken from a study of Fr. Arij A. Roest Crollius, who, in turn, seems to take his inspiration from the letter of Fr. Arrupe on inculturation: "The inculturation of the Church is the integration of the Christian experience of a local Church into the culture of its people, in such a way that this experience not only express itself in elements of this culture, but becomes a force that animates, orients and innovates this culture so as to create a new unity and communion, not only within the culture in question but also as an enrichment of the Church universal".[9]

These two descriptions seem to agree in pointing out two elements of inculturation. First of all, it is a process of integration

---

[8] Final Statement of the Second Plenary Assembly of the FABC, n. 31, in: *FABC Papers*, n° 13, p. 20.

[9] Arij A. ROEST CROLLIUS, *What is so new about inculturation? A concept and its implications*, in: *Gregorianum*, 59 (1978), 735; cf. id., *Per una teologia pratica dell'inculturazione*, in: *Inculturazione. Concetti, Problemi, Orientamenti*, Centrum Ignatianum Spiritualitatis, Roma, 1979, p. 37.

which is profound and organic, and not a syncretism or simply a coexistence. Secondly, this integration is expressed as a new creation, something new to the culture and to the Christian life as well.

It seems to me that precisely these two essential aspects of inculturation are lacking in the approach which considers Zen as a preparation for prayer. In this approach, Zen forms and Christian prayer coexist as independent entities. On the other hand, the two traditions, Zen and Christian prayer, are not innovated "to create a new unity and communion".[10]

Inculturation goes through a process of three stages: that of assumption, that of transformation and that of bearing fruit in a new synthesis.[11] Looking at inculturation as process, this approach can be collocated in the first phase, that is, the phase of assumption. Yet a question can still be put to this approach: Is it open to enter into the second phase of transformation? It seems to me that, in practice, this approach does not have a dynamic tension; it rather stands by itself, and is not as a phase in a process.

2. *Zen-practice as a way of dialogue*

There are Christians today who are practising Zen as a way of dialogue with Buddhists. They practise Zen in order to penetrate into the Buddhist experience of meditation, in order to understand it, to compare it with the Christian experience and to share Christian values with Buddhists.

At the basis of this approach is the situation of the dialogue. At present, the dialogue between Catholics and Buddhists on the philosophical or theological level seems to be at a deadlock because of the lack of a common terminology, and because of the wide gap existing between the two visions.[12]

This situation can be explained existentially by a personal experience of Fr. William Johnston: "In the hot summer of 1968 I had the privilege of participating in the Zen-Christian dialogue held

---

[10] Arij A. ROEST CROLLIUS, *What is so new about inculturation? A concept and its implications*, p. 735.

[11] Cf. Arij A. ROEST CROLLIUS, *Per una teologia pratica dell'inculturazione*, p. 39.

[12] Cf. Dinh Duc DAO, *Prayer and Evangelization*, in: *My witnesses. Missionary Spirituality*, Centro Internazionale di Animazione Missionaria, Roma, 1982, p. 106.

in Kyoto. This was an unforgettable experience — a week in which Buddhists and Christians met in an atmosphere of great cordiality, forming deep friendships and laying the foundations for further union. Obviously we were not in complete accord on every point. On the contrary, when it came to formulating propositions on which we agreed, it seemed that there was not a single philosophical or theological tenet that we held in common. An unbridgeable gulf appeared to separate those who believed in the soul, the Absolute, and the objectivity of truth from those who spoke of nirvana, nothingness and the void".[13]

This situation gave rise to a new way of carrying on dialogue, that is, dialogue on the profound level of religious experience. The Christian contemplatives in Asia, in their meeting at Bangkok in 1968, all agreed on the necessity of a dialogue on this level of religious experience. Since then, there have been many meetings between Christian contemplatives and Buddhist monks, where they not only discussed but also shared their experiences of contemplation.[14]

However, many are not satisfied with what they hear about Zen meditation; they want to understand from within, to have a direct and personal experience of Zen so that they can enter into a more fruitful dialogue with their Buddhist interlocutors.

As we can see, strictly speaking, this approach does not aim at inculturation. Its direct interest is not the integration of Zen meditation in the prayer-life of the Christian, but the authentic understanding of the Buddhist experience in view of dialogue. Even so, indirectly this approach can help a great deal to further the process of the inculturation of Zen meditation in the prayer-life of the Christian. In fact, one can assume an element only if one understands correctly its meanings and its values. Therefore, in this approach Zen practice can be collocated in the first stage of the process of the inculturation.

3. Zen as a form of Christian prayer

Different from the preceding approaches, which look on Zen and Christian prayer as two distinct realities while recognising that

---

[13] William JOHNSTON, *The Still Point*, Fordham University Press, New York, 1982, Preface, p. xiii.
[14] Cf. Dinh Duc DAO, *Prayer and Evangelization*, p. 107.

they may have points in common, this approach tends to identify them. Zen is considered as a form of Christian prayer. To follow the Zen way is to pray as a Christian. Thus, today, there are Christians who are practising Zen under the direction of a Buddhist master and they are going through the Zen "koan";[15] others are attending "retreats" conducted by Buddhist masters.[16] In this way, Zen is accepted totally as it is into Christian life.

This approach seems to raise serious questions. First of all, in regard to the process of inculturation, a direct assumption of Zen seems to be a hasty step. As has been mentioned above, inculturation is a profound and organic integration into Christian life of the values existing in the cultures of the people. This approach, however, does not offer an integration; instead of integration, we have rather the identification of Zen with Christian prayer. In fact, this approach seems to reflect a spiritual situation of modern man rather than an effort to achieve real inculturation.

The modern world and particularly the Western world, in spite of its magnificence and its many scientific miracles, seems to be uneasy with its spiritual poverty. We are living in a brave new world of robots. At the same time, the Christian life has become too rational, too juridical and deprived of its mystical dimension. It is in this context of life that Zen Buddhism has made an appearance offering precisely the values which modern man seems to lack. "Not a few Westerners have turned their eyes to Zen in search of something profound that may be able to satisfy their deeper aspirations".[17]

This situation raises the second question which concerns the direct transplantation of Zen into the Western world. Is it possible for the Westerner to practise Zen rigorously as it is?

It seems to me that because of the difference of the mental education and of the vision of life, a direct transplantation of Zen to the West is very problematic, perhaps impossible, although Zen may be of great value for some particular individual Westerner. Dr. Takeo Doi maintains that "lonely Western man has developed his

---

[15] Cf. William JOHNSTON, Zen – The present situation, p. 344.

[16] Thomas B. O'GORMAN, A Pastoral Seminar on Asian forms of Prayer, in: EAPR, 20 (1983), 338.

[17] William JOHNSTON, The Still Point, p. 171-172; cf. Henri CAFFAREL, Il nostro mondo cerca esperienza di preghiera, in: Mondo e Missione, 104 (1975), 277-280.

ego too much, finds that he can no longer cope with the situation he has created, feels an ever-growing insecurity, and looks for a solution in the non-ego condition of Zen. He seems to think that Zen is healthy if one breaks through to 'satori'. But many do not. Instead, they break down mentally".[18] This result is not just a hypothesis, but it is a fact which can be proved by experience.[19]

However, there are among those who follow this approach many who are not Westerners; they are Asian Christians. Hence, all the above difficulties would disappear. This could be true, but this does not mean that there is no problem. In this case the problem is raised on the more profound level of religious experience. I would like to approach it under two aspects, that is, methods and essence of mysticism.

The Zen way is essentially the way of detachment: detachment from everything, even from thoughts, images, desires, hopes and fears; finally, one must be detached from one's very self. All this will lead to a great interior silence (*silentium mysticum*), which brings about an extraordinary psychic integration in which one may obtain the true wisdom.

We also have the long tradition of Christian mysticism represented particularly by Dionysius, by the anonymous author of "The Cloud of Unknowing" and by St John of the Cross, which gives much importance to detachment. The soul that wishes to enter into the divine union should be free from all things of whatever kind. This radical detachment leads to the *silentium mysticum*.

Thus, the two ways, Zen and Christian, are one in teaching detachment. However, the Christian tradition differs radically on its teaching about the foundation of detachment, which St John of the Cross calls "the living flame of love". It is precisely to nourish this living flame of love, "to let it develop and grow, that detachment is practised; for this secret little love must become a raging fire that envelops the whole personality and governs every action of one's life.... If Christian contemplation demands a total detachment and abnegation, this is precisely for the living flame of love".[20]

---

[18] Cf. William JOHNSTON, *the Still Point*, p. 176.

[19] Cf. Adriano PELOSIN, *Thailandia: primi passi con Buddha*, in: *Mondo e Missione*, 113 (1984), 243-266.

[20] William JOHNSTON, *Zen and Christian contemplation*, in: *Review for Religious*, 29 (1970), 701.

No such teaching on the living flame of love can be found in Zen. Yet, this is the very center and essence of Christian contemplation. Thus, Zen and Christian contemplation may be similar in forms of prayer, but they differ widely in content and perspectives.[21] This will become even clearer if we now examine the meaning of mysticism.

Mysticism is the very center of the Christian faith and Zen Buddhism. According to Louis Bouyer, Christian mysticism in its origin is associated with "mystery", particularly as found in the Pauline teaching, that is, the mystery of Christ, the center of which is the mystery of the Cross, "to the Jews, an obstacle they cannot get over, to the pagans, madness, but to those who have been called, whether they are Jews or Greeks, a Christ who is the power and the wisdom of God" (1 Cor 1:24).

To enter into mysticism is to enter into the mystery of Christ, but one cannot enter deeply into the mystery of Christ only by using words and images, by reasoning and thinking. "It may rather be an entering into the *silentium mysticum* where I rest in the mystery and remain present to the mystery. Indeed, this presence may be so deep and unfamiliar that it seems like absence".[22]

From this consideration, I would like to draw a conclusion: an orthodox Christian mysticism must be centered on the mystery of Christ. To enter into mystical experience is to enter into the mystery of Christ where one meets the Father. For this reason, the peak of the mystical experience is described as mystical union or marriage. Moreover, centered on the mystery of Christ, Christian mysticism cannot be separated from the Eucharist, from the Scriptures and from the Church, His Body.

The Zen experience too is centered on mysticism in the sense that it is supraconceptual and it emphasizes silence, emptiness and nothingness. It is not sufficient just to sit in the lotus posture, to chant the koan "Mu", and to concentrate one's mind in order to attain this stillness and inner silence and to reach enlightenment. The Zen experience requires something more than techniques. It requires a very great faith in the sense that some modern theologians give to it, that is, a total commitment and trust. The

---

[21] Yves RAGUIN, *Christianity and Zen*, in: *EAPR*, 20 (1983), 345.
[22] William JOHNSTON, *Zen – The present situation*, p. 341.

techniques must be practised with the sustenance of a faith, expressed in the words chanted constantly in the temple:

> I surrender to the Buddha
> I surrender to the dharma
> I surrender to the sangha

This does not necessarily mean that one must put total commitment and trust in Buddha as God and Saviour in the Christian perspective, but one must commit oneself totally to the way taught by Buddha, trusting that his way is the right one to lead to enlightenment through which comes salvation. For this reason, I doubt that those who practise Zen only as methods can ever get to the heart of Zen experience.

There is certainly the objection raised by the koan "Mu" (nothing). Nothing, absolutely nothing. For this reason, it is taught that during meditation, if you meet the Buddha on the way, you must kill the Buddha. In fact, this teaching has created much confusion and misunderstanding. Sometimes, Buddjhism is presented as a type of nihilism. Nothing, absolutely nothing. Basing myself on a Zen master, Hui-Neng, the sixth Patriarch of Chinese Zen, heir of a long tradition, of which the origin was the Buddha himself, I would put the matter in this way: the Zen way consists in the absence of thought, meditation without object, simply facing "Original Nature", and not relying-on, not dwelling-in.[23] In this perspective, the koan "Mu" should be understood not in the metaphysical, but in the phenomenological order.

Thus, there is a faith which underlies the Zen experience. Indeed, one cannot throw oneself totally into the way if one does not believe firmly that this is the right way which leads to enlightenment, and that through enlightenment one can get salvation. It is precisely this point which separates the Zen and Christian ways. From the phenomenological and psychological point of view, the religious experience in Zen and Christian mysticism is very similar, but the content is quite different, because its foundation that is, the faith which underlies it is different.

Considering the radical difference in the very foundation, a direct acceptance of Zen as it is into the Christian life certainly creates serious problems.

---

[23] Yves RAGUIN, *Christianity and Zen*, p. 345-346.

4. *The Zen form adapted in the Christian perspective*

In this approach to Zen, one prays following Zen methods creatively, and, if necessary, a Christian content is given to it. Thus, many Christians are learning to sit in the lotus or half-lotus posture. Sometimes they just sit quietly before the Blessed Sacrament; sometimes they repeat a phrase taken from the Gospels. This is a way of using koan (Buddhist method) with Christian content. In adopting Zen forms, this approach is somewhat similar to the first approach which looks on Zen as a preparation for prayer. But it is in fact different, because this approach does not look on Zen only as a preparation for prayer, but transforms Zen into a Christian prayer.

This approach seems to be a good way to integrate Zen into the Christian life. However, at present, we are far from being before a fulfilled task. The efforts which have been made are rather experiments which should be encouraged so that a new synthesis may come about to enrich the Christian prayer-life.

This brief survey on the efforts which have been made to integrate the Christian prayer-life with Zen tradition clearly shows that the process of inculturation is not an easy one. In fact, according to the witness of Fr. Thomas H. O'Gorman, "there have been cases of Jesuits who after some in-depth exposure to forms of traditional Asian spiritualities, have not found the process of integration an easy one".[24]

On the other hand, in spite of the fact that there has been a growing interest in the integration of Zen into the Christian prayer-life, this is not yet an effort of the whole local church of Asia. The Third Plenary Assembly of the FABC in 1982 acknowledged this situation in the following way: "Although in recent years much progress has been made in formation to, and exercise of prayer, still much remains to be done toward fostering it in our communities. Sometimes there is little or no prayer even in religious houses. Priests and religious do not do enough to help their fellow-Christians in the practice of prayer. Our ecclesial communities often are lacking that esteem for spiritual values which are so highly regarded in Asia, especially by many Asian religions and their adherents".[25]

---

[24] Thomas H. O'Gorman, *A Pastoral Seminar on Asian forms of Prayer*, p. 339.

[25] Statement of the third Plenary Assembly of the FABC, Samphran (Thailand), 20-28 October, 1982, n. 9.5, in: *EAPR*, 20(1983), 36.

After these considerations, one further question can be raised: What needs to be done to foster the process of integrating Zen meditation into the Christian prayer-life? The question is a big one, and I shall attempt a very modest answer. I mean that I will not venture to formulate a global answer to the question, but will try only to point out some aspects which could serve as a suggestion for further research.

III. Towards a Christian Zen

In the writings on the inculturation of prayer in Asia, there are references to "Christian Zen". This is a form of contemplation in which the values of Zen meditation are harmoniously integrated, although it remains fully Christian. The effort of inculturation must aim at this integration to infuse a new vein into the prayer-life of the churches in Asia.

When the inculturation of Zen into the Christian life is discussed, it is often asked to what extent Zen meditation can be introduced into Christian prayer. It is difficult to venture an answer at this moment. The various experiences to date, which have been summarized in the above four approaches, are proof of this. However, we can be sure that when Zen meditation is finally integrated, the life of the churches in Asia will be infused with a new vitality.

These considerations give hope for the continuation of efforts toward inculturation and, at the same time, they turn our attention to a more practical side of the question.

In order to determine the field for reflection, it is necessary to keep in mind the distinction of inculturation as process and as praxis. Inculturation as *process* refers rather to the collective and historical aspect of the integration of the Christian experience into a culture, while inculturation as *praxis* refers to the responsibility of the Christian in the process of inculturation.[26] With regard to inculturation as process, the question is "What needs to be done?", while the question asked in relation to inculturation as praxis is "What are the attitudes of the Christian?".

---

[26] Cf. Arij A. Roest Crollius, Per una teologia pratica dell'inculturazione, p. 37.

The distinction of inculturation as process and praxis, with the respective interrogatives, opens up two avenues for reflection: one concerns the role of contemplation in the Christian life, and the other concerns the spirituality of the agents of inculturation.

1. *Renewal of contemplation in the Christian life*

Since Vatican II, there has been renewal in many aspects of the life of the Church: modification of edifices; new style of music in liturgy; new forms of ecclesial communities; renewal courses on pastoral and theology, etc.

All these efforts are excellent, but they will be similar to a house built on sand if renewal does not enter into its very heart, that is, into the mystical level. In this respect, one should mention the presence of schools of prayer, the movements of prayer groups, of retreats and spiritual exercises which in one way or another introduce the Christian into contemplative prayer. For the churches in Asia, the efforts to integrate Zen meditation into the Christian prayer-life provide an additional reason to renew contemplative prayer in the life of the Church.

Zen meditation is situated precisely at the level of contemplative prayer in the Christian life. Therefore, the first question which the effort at inculturation should raise is about the value of contemplation in the Christian life: What is the role of contemplation in the life of the Christian?

The problem must be examined not only on the level of principle, but also on the level of reality. Precisely at this level, there seems to be a certain difficulty in the life of the Church. For a long time, contemplative prayer has been considered as a form of prayer reserved for monks and as something extraneous to the ordinary Christian. These recent years have seen the awakening in the Church of a certain interest in contemplation, and the form of contemplative prayer has been introduced into the life of many Christians through schools of prayer, prayer groups and retreat movements. However, it remains a fact that contemplative prayer is still limited to the groups and movements, while the majority of Christians do not practise it.

This situation can be explained to some extent by the story related by Fr. William Johnston. Today, contemplation interests scientists too. In the USA and in Japan, researchers are using machines to measure the brainwaves and biofeedback of contemplatives during contemplation. "As the researchers kindly told me about their tests with *roshi* and *swami* and various *gurus* from the East, I asked in a flash of Irish chauvinism why they didn't test some Christian monks. They replied that they did. They tested some Catholic clergymen. But whereas the yogis and masters sat silently in majestic splendour registering exquisite and impeccable alpha,[27] the clergymen read the Bible, sang hymns, wandered around the room and fouled up the machines.... Undismayed, however, I reflected that they may have asked the wrong people, and I suggested that they experiment with Cistercian or Carthusian monks who have a long tradition of silent and imageless meditation...."[28]

One should not generalize a situation. However, the above story seems to reflect the state of contemplative prayer in the life of the Church. Therefore, the integration of Zen meditation into the Christian life requires, above all, the effort to rediscover the value and the place of contemplation in the Christian life. The integration of Zen meditation will not be possible, or will at least be very difficult, if contemplation has no place in the Christian life.

It is necessary to rediscover that contemplation is not something reserved exclusively to monks, but is the vocation of every Christian, although there are different degrees of practising it. While monks consecrate their life to contemplation, other Christians are called to dedicate some moment of the day to contemplation. If contemplative prayer is not appreciated by Christians, and if it is not accepted as an integral element of their Christian life, the integration of Zen meditation will remain a theoretical discussion among specialists and, at best, it will be practised by a group of elites.

There is another aspect of the renewal of contemplation in the Christian life, that is, the form of contemplation. Zen meditation

---

[27] There are 4 principal brainwaves: *Beta* is the most common in our waking hours; *Alpha* is more restful and reflects interior silence; *Theta* is associated with drowsiness; *Delta* is the rhythm found in deep sleep.

[28] William JOHNSTON, *Silent Music. The Science of Meditation,* Collins, Fount Paperbacks, 1983, p. 36-37.

can be an obstacle for many people because of its meditation form, which is presented as a meditation without emotion, without thought, without image. This way of meditation without object seems very negative, strange and unchristian; hence, it causes no little reluctance among Christians who want to approach Zen.

However, what looks strange and unchristian in Zen medication is not completely alien to the Christian tradition which can be traced, at least, from Dionysius through the anonymous author of *The Cloud of Unknowing,* to the mystics of the Rhineland and St John of the Cross. The author of *The Cloud of Unknowing* advised his disciple to empty every thought and image from his mind, but fill it with faith, while St John of the Cross recommended a radical detachment from everything: concept, image, desire, etc. The soul that seeks to enter the divine union should be free from all desires, however slight they may be.

Thus, the integration of Zen meditation into the Christian prayer-life certainly requires a thorough understanding of Zen forms of meditation and their meanings. At the same time, it also requires research into Christian tradition to rediscover those forms of prayer which are present, but forgotten and neglected in our time.

A profound understanding of both the Christian and Zen traditions is necessary if we want to work out any true synthesis, for one cannot build a house on nothing. For this reason, we should be grateful to the comparative studies of Zen and Christian mysticism done by Fr. Hugo Enomiya Lassalle, Fr. William Johnston, Dom Aelrel Graham, Fr. Ichiro Okumura, Fr. J. Kakichi Kadowaki and others.[29] Much has been done, but much still remains to be completed.

2. *Spirituality for inculturation*

While inculturation as *process* requires a reflection on the concrete steps which should be taken so that the integration of the

---

[29] H. Enomiya Lassalle, *Zen Meditation for Christians,* Open Court, 1974; W. Johnston, *Christian Zen,* Harper and Row, 1971; Id., *The Still Point,* Fordham University Press, New York, 1982; Aelred Graham, *Zen Catholicism,* Harcourt, Brace and World, 1963; I. Okumura, *The Christian contribution to the life of prayer in the Church of Asia,* in: *FABC Papers,* n° 10; J. Karichi Kadowari, *Zen and the Bible. A Priest's Experience,* Sophia University, Tokyo (Italian transl.: *Lo Zen e la Bibbia,* Paoline, Milano, 1985).

Gospel in a culture can be brought about, inculturation as *praxis* points out the responsibility of the Christian in this process. The inculturation of the Gospel does not come about without the collaboration of Christians as individuals and as communities. Therefore, inculturation as praxis requires an appropriate formation for Christians in general, and in particular for those apostles who are called to operate directly in the field of inculturation.[30]

The formation of Christians with a view to inculturation should embrace all the aspects involved in this process. However, the interiority of the Christian seems to require special attention, because the efforts of a person depend a great deal on the interior attitudes rooted in his heart. This means that we are entering the field of spirituality. However, this reflection does not pretend to give a comprehensive spirituality for inculturation, but only tries modestly to point out a few spiritual attitudes which seem necessary and urgent for the task of inculturation.[31]

a) *In the light of the mystery of the Holy Trinity*

Inculturation should not be thought of merely as an anthropological or sociological need, but as a truly theological issue; it is not simply a tactic for the propagation of the faith, but belongs to the very core of evangelization, being rooted in the mystery of redemption.[32] Reflection on inculturation should therefore be done in the light of the mission of the Church.

According to the Second Vatican Council, the mission of the Church has its origin in the mission of the Son and the mission of the Holy Spirit, in accordance with the plan which flows from the fountain of love within the Father (AG 2). Thus, going to the roots of the mission of the Church, we find ourselves face to face with the inscrutable mystery of the love and the life of the Holy Trinity; and before it one should remain silent in contemplation so

---

[30] The First Bishops' Institute for Missionary Apostolate of the FABC (BIMA I), in: *FABC Papers*, n° 19, p. 9.

[31] One of the most recommended studies of this kind is the study of Fr. Arij A. ROEST CROLLIUS: *Per una teologia pratica dell'inculturazione*, in: *Inculturazione. Concetti, Problemi, Orientamenti*, Centrum Ignatianum Spiritualitatis, Roma, 1979, p. 36-53.

[32] BIMA I, in: *FABC Papers*, n° 19, p. 8-9.

as to be fully immersed in this unfathomable mystery and taken up fully by it.[33]

Rooted in the mystery of the Holy Trinity, the mission of the Church requires that the missionary must, first of all, be grasped by God in order to be identified with him. Between God and the missionary in his mission, there is a relationship of intimacy and conformity. The preached mystery is the contemplated mystery. Contemplation is mission at its source, while mission is contemplation in action. Paradoxically the Church is most active and most authentic in her mission when she enters into contemplation.

Collocated in this vision of the mission of the Church, inculturation is not simply the application of an intellectual reflection, but the fruit of a spiritual insight, rooted in the mystery of the love and the life of God. When a missionary is immersed in and grasped by the mystery of God, there is a breaking up of boundaries in his mind and his heart so that he sees the reality as it is in the salvific plan of God.

Thus, the spirituality for inculturation is, first of all, a spirituality of *silence* and *contemplation*. The contemplative spirit is necessary, not simply because of a need to make the message more acceptable for the mystics of our time, or as a quality required in order to be able to enter into a dialogue with them, but it is required by the very nature of inculturation. Contemplation is the point where the process of inculturation starts.

The mystery of the Holy Trinity is the mystery of the comunity of three divine Persons, united in a communion from which flows the mission of the Church. The trinitarian origin of the mission requires an attitude of respect for persons with their legitimate differences. The possibility of pluralism of cultures in the unity of the Church is intimately linked to the trinitarian concept of man, as person with other persons. Without the trinitarian concept of man in community, one can only have an acculturation to one sole way of being Church and being man,[34] and inculturation becomes

---

[33] Cf. Adolfo DE NICOLAS, *Formation and Spirituality for Mission*, in: *Toward a New Age in Mission*. International Congress on Mission, Book Three, IMC, Manila, 1981, p. 221.

[34] Cf. Arij A. ROEST CROLLIUS, *Per una teologia pratica dell'inculturazione*, p. 50.

uniformity or source of division However, in the light of the community of the Holy Trinity one should appreciate the differences as an opportunity for *communion* which enriches everybody because, in communion among persons, nobody lives only for himself; each person's originality and identity is always a gift which is given and received, never a property to be defended and kept jealously.[35]

There is another aspect of the mystery of the Holy Trinity in relation to the spirituality for inculturation. The communion which has been mentioned is communion in the Holy Spirit, who is not the spirit of slaves bringing fear, but the Spirit of sons, making us cry out "Abba, Father" (cf. Rom 8:15), and who has poured into our hearts the love of God (cf. Rom 5:5) which overcomes the law of the flesh. Thus, a spirituality for inculturation is a spirituality of openness to the Holy Spirit who leads us to the *interior freedom* without which the Christian will easily run the risk of falling again into a new particularism. This would mean starting with the Spirit and finishing with the flesh (cf. Gal 3:3).[36] But it is not worth fighting against one particularism only to fall into another particularism.

b) *In the light of the mystery of Christ*

It is declared in the Final Statement of the Second Plenary Assembly of the FABC that "in keeping with the economy of the Incarnation, which is the law of the Church's life and mission, the prayer-life of our local churches should take over the riches of our nations, which have been given to Christ as an inheritance".[37]

The mystery of the Incarnation is usually accepted as the criterion and model of inculturation. However, the Incarnation must be understood in its full dimension and perspective. First of all, in the mystery of the Incarnation, Christ has assumed full humanity, except for sin. Therefore, in the light of the Incarnation one should appreciate what is good in every culture. This requires a great *openness of mind and heart,* and particularly *wisdom,* in order to discern the true value existing in every culture.

---

[35] *Ibidem.*

[36] *Ibidem,* p. 43.

[37] Final Statement of the Second Plenary Assembly of the FABC, n. 30, in: *FABC Papers,* n° 13, p. 19.

Secondly, in the Incarnation, Christ did not simply assume humanity, but assumed humanity to purify, transform and redeem it. The Son of God became man, so that man might become God; God is humanized so that man may be divinized. This aspect of the Incarnation means, for Christ, a process of emptying Himself in order to share the same condition as every person: "His state was divine, yet he did not cling to his equality with God, but emptied himself to assume the condition of a slave" (Phil 2:6-7).

Thirdly, the mystery of the Incarnation cannot be understood as an isolated reality. In its dynamic aspect, the mystery of the Incarnation is so intimately related to the Paschal mystery, that the mystery of the Incarnation cannot be understood without the Paschal mystery and viceversa (cf. Phil 2:6-11). In the light of the letter to the Philippians, they are, rather, two complementary aspects of the same movement which is the infinite love of God who wants to save mankind. In the Incarnation, love manifests itself as an act of sharing, participating and assuming the condition of every man; in the Paschal mystery, love is manifested in the act of donation and of self-giving even to the supreme act of oblation as victim of love.

In the light of the mystery of the Incarnation understood in a close relationship with the mystery of the Cross, the style of the Christian who works for inculturation is that of *love* and *service* in the manner of Christ, the humble Servant, who accepts even *emptying himself* to assume the *emptying* condition of a slave, and responding to the ultimate demand of love in the gift of himself by death on the Cross.

For authentic inculturation, it is necessary to have the presence of those "professional slaves of love", who make a profession of obedience like that of Christ and who are always animated by unconditional love and respect for every person in his own reality, especially for the poor and small ones, accepting the weight of the tension between purely human efficiency and evangelical love.[38] Thanks to such service of love, the cultures of humanity will be transformed so that the Gospel of Christ may be at home everywhere.

---

[37] Cf. Arij A. ROEST CROLLIUS, *Per una teologia pratica dell'inculturazione*, p. 48.

166

c) *In the light of the mystery of the Church*

In explaining the mystery of the Church, the Second Vatican Council makes use of many images: the Church is a sheepfold, a land cultivated by God, a house of God, a temple, the spouse of the Lamb, the Body of Christ, the People of God (cf. LG 6 & 9).

One can observe among these images and even within every image, a certain tension between oneness and plurality, between stability and progress, between preservation and growth. This tension indicates that inculturation is not something extraneous to the Church. On the contrary, it belongs to her very nature as mystery.

Among all the images which explain the mystery of the Church, perhaps the image of the Church as the People of God in constant pilgrimage towards the Father's house can give the clearest indication for a spirituality for inculturation.

The People advancing towards the Promised Land must constantly keep moving forward. On the way, they are invited to abandon their heritage of Egypt to adapt themselves to the new conditions of life, only to discover, at the end, that they must enter into the desert, abandoning everything, in order to possess the Promised Land. The spirit of desert is a spirit of purification, of detachment and of radical freedom in order to give attention only to the essential; all the rest is relative.

In the light of the Church as a people on pilgrimage, a spirituality for inculturation is a spirituality of *exodus* and of *desert*. Those who work in the field of inculturation are called to live in radical detachment, accepting the condition of not having a home, even culturally. Everywhere they are like pilgrims, who acknowledge modestly and accept joyfully the condition of their cultural poverty, not being able to have anything as their "own", often not even a language.[39] This, however, seems to be a rule of the evangelical paradox: he who wants to preserve his life will lose it; he who accepts losing his life for Christ's sake will find it (cf. Mt 10:39). Only he who is free from his own culture can properly appreciate his culture and that of others. The attitude of exodus and desert helps the Christian to become all for all and, at the same time, to have a critical attitude before the tendencies that exist in a culture to close itself in it own particularism.

---

[39] *Ibidem*, p. 43.

When one discusses inculturation in Asia, one often complains that the work of inculturation is hindered because its leaders have been formed in Europe or America. However, the formation abroad should not necessarily be negative for the work of inculturation. On the contrary, in the light of the above consideration on the spirituality of exodus and desert, the formation abroad could be positive and even necessary. It is negative only when the person substitutes his own culture with another one, transforming it into an idol.

There is still another aspect of the mystery of the Church as the People of God, which requires reflection. The People of God is one, but the functions of its members are many and different. If there are members who work to consolidate the People, there are members who work at the frontiers so that the People may move forward on its pilgrimage. Although all the People are pilgrims, there are members who live the pilgrimage as their personal vocation. They are pioneers who must explore new lands for the People. This means that research for the inculturation of the Gospel must be seen in a global perspective as a service for the whole People, and not simply as a need of one person or one particular group. For this wide scope of inculturation, a profound spirit of *humility* and *ecclesial communion* is required so that the work of inculturation may be a service for the progress of the whole Church, and not carried out for its own sake, as a manifestation of cultural pride.

At the conclusion of this study, not much is left to be said, except on the necessity to encourage all efforts to renew contemplative prayer in the life of the Church in Asia through the inculturation of Zen meditation. The civilization of technology which has moulded modern societies is spreading all over the countries of Asia.

Paradoxically, modern technology has helped to awaken a renewed interest in the profound dimension of life, as is manifested in the movements concerned with meditation. At present, thousands of people are searching for interior peace through Zen, Yoga and Transcendental Meditation. This phenomenon is certainly a challenge for the Church in her mission. What is happening in the more advanced societies is happening in Asian societies too, and will do so even more clearly in the near future. Therefore, more efforts should be made to renew contemplation in the Christian life so that the churches in Asia will be prepared to face this challenge.

JOSEPH DINH DUC DAO

BIBLIOGRAPHY

1. Statements of the FABC

FABC I, *Evangelization in the Modern Day Asia*. Statement and Recommendations of the First Plenary Assembly of the FABC, Taipei, 27th April, 1974, in: *FABC Papers*, n°28, p. 14-25.

FABC II, *Prayer – The Life of the Church of Asia*. Final Statement and Recommendations of the Second Plenary Assembly of the FABC, Calcutta, 25th November, 1978, in: *FABC Papers*, n°13.

FABC II, *Prayer, Community Worship and Inculturation*. Worshop discussion guide, in: *FABC Papers*, n°12f.

FABC III, *The Church – A community of Faith in Asia*. A short Report on the Third Plenary Assembly of the FABC, Samphran (Thailand), 28th October, 1982, in: *FABC Papers*, n°32; cf. *EAPR*, 20 (1983), 31-39.

BIMA I, Report of the First Bishops' Institute for Missionary Apostolate of the FABC, in: *FABC Papers*, n°19.

2. Books and Articles

AMALADOSS M., *Sadhana: Marges and methods*, in: *Vidyajyoti*, 42 (1978), 414-422.

AMALADOSS M., *Forms of prayer. Some reflection in the context of Hindu-Christian dialogue*, in: *Vidyajyoti*, 39 (1975), 430-440.

AMALADOSS M., *Inculturation and Tasks of Mission*, in: *Toward a new Age in Mission*. International Congress on Mission, Book Three, Position Papers, IMC, Manila, 1981, p. 33-45.

AMALORPAVADASS D.S., *New Theological Approaches in Asia* (With reference to Religions and Cultures other than Western Culture and Christianity), in: *Verbum SVD*, 1980, p. 279302.

AMALORPAVADASS D.S., *Gospel and Culture*, in: *FABC Papers*, n°15.

ANAND S., *The Universal call to contemplation*, in: *Vidyajyoti*, 41 (1977), 414-448.

BULATAO J., *Praying in an altered state of consciousness*, in: *EAPR*, 20 (1983), 357-362.

BULATAO J., REILLY J., WILCKEN J., CLAVER F.F., *Inculturating Christianity in East Asia*, in: *FABC Papers*, n°7, p. 18-35.

169

CAFFAREL H., *Il nostro mondo cerca esperienza di preghiera*, in: *Mondo e Missione*, 104 (1975), 277-280.

CAFFAREL H., *Si cercano "guru" per la Chiesa*, in: *Mondo e Missione*, 104 (1975), 345-348.

CLARK F.X., *Inculturation: Introduction and History*, in: *Teaching all Nations*, 15 (1978), 211-225.

CLARK F.X., *Making the Gospel at home in Asian cultures: some questions, suggestions, hopes*, in: *Teaching all Nations*, 13 (1976), 131-149.

DE MELLO A., *Sadhana, a way to God*, Gujarat Sahitya Prakash, Anand (India), 1978.

DHAVAMONY M. (director), *Meditation in Christianity and other Religions*. Stiudia Missionalia 25, Gregorian University Press, Rome, 1876.

DHAVAMONY M. (director), *Mystique dans le Christianisme et les autres Religions*. Studia Missionalia 26, Gregorian University Press, Rome, 1977.

Dinh Duc DAO, *Prayer and Evangelization*, in: *My Witnesses...*, ESQUERDA BIFET J., et al., Centro Internazionale di Animazione Missionaria, Roma, 1982, p. 97-117.

DIVARKAR P.R., *Reflections on the problem of Inculturation*, in: *FABC Papers*, n° 7, p. 1-8.

EK THABPING J., *The conversion of Thai Buddhists: are Christianity and Thai culture irreconciable?* (Thesis presented for the Degree of Master of Arts), Graduate School, Ateneo de Manila University, 1974.

ENOMIYA LASSALLE H., *Zen Meditation for Christians*, La Salle, Open Court, 1974.

ENOMIYA LASSALLE H., *Méditation Zen et prière Chrétienne*, Cerf, Paris, 1973.

GARDINI W., *Un'esperienza di meditazione Zen a Kyoto*, in: *Mondo e Missione*, 107 (1978), 397-404.

GENTILI A., *Un corso di meditazione Buddhista Mahayana*, in: *Mondo e Missione*, 105 (1976), 196-199.

GENTILI A., *Il ritiro Zen. Una nuova forma di Esercizi Spirituali*, in: *Mondo e Missione*, 108 (1979), 546-548.

GRIFFITHS B., *Indian Christian contemplation*, in: *The Clergy Monthly*, August 1971, p. 277-281.

HABITO R.L.F., *A Christian reflects on his Zen experience*, in: *EAPR*, 20 (1983), 351-352.

HARDAWIRYANA R.H., *The Growing Church: amid various religious and cultural Traditions and contemporary ideologies. The Ecumenical Task in Asia*, in: *FABC Papers*, n° 14.

HIRYDAYAM I., *Prayer in Asian Traditions*, in: *FABC Papers*, n° 11.

JOHNSTON W., *Christian Zen*, Gill and MacMillan, Dublin, 1979.

JOHNSTON W., *The Still Point*, Fordham University Press, New York, 1970.

JOHNSTON W., *Silent Music*, Collins, Fount Paperbacks, Bungaj, Suffolk, 7th impression, 1983.

JOHNSTON W., *Zen: the present situation*, in: *EAPR*, 20 (1983), 340-344.

JOHNSTON W., *Zen and Christian contemplation*, in: *Review for Religious*, 29 (1970), 699-704.

KAKICHI KADOWAKI J., *Zen and the Bible. A Priest's Experience*, Sophia University, Tokyo.

LOPEZ-GAY J., *Mistica oriental y busqueda del Dios Trinitario*, in: *Estudios Trinitarios*, 16 (1980), 542-561.

LOPEZ-GAY J., *Pensiero attuale della Chiesa sull'inculturazione*, in: *Inculturazione. Concetti, problemi, orientamenti*, Centrum Ignatianum Spiritualitatis, Roma, 1979, p. 9-35.

NEDUNGATT G., *Il processo e i problemi dell'inculturazione visti dall'Est*, in: *Inculturazione. Concetti, problemi, orientamenti*, Centrum Ignatianum Spiritualitatis, Roma, 1979, p. 89-121.

NICOLAS A., *Formation and Spirituality for Mission*, in: *Toward a New Age in Mission*. International Congress on Mission, Book Three, IMC, Manila, 1981, p. 217-237; also in: *EAPR*, 17 (1980), 104-116, 142.

OKUMURA A.I., *Différence entre méditation Zen et prière Chrétienne*, in: *Omnis Terra*, 22 (1983), 151-155.

OKUMURA A.I., *The Christian contribution to the life of prayer in the Church of Asia*, in: *FABC Papers*, n° 10.

PELOSIN A., *Thailandia: primi passi con Budda* (Intervistato da CERVELLERA B.), in: *Mondo e Missione*, 113 (1984), 243-266.

RAGUIN Y., *Christianity and Zen*, in: *EAPR*, 20 (1983), 345-350.

RATNA BAMRUNGTRAKUL R., *Inculturation and Mission*, in: *Omnis Terra*, 17 (1983), 319-323.

RATNA BAMRUNGTRAKUL R., *You can change yourself and the world with Christian-Asian meditation*, in: *Omnia Terra*, 16 (1982), 145-150.

RATNA BAMRUNGTRAKUL R., *Christian-Asian meditation: a contribution to the life of the Church*, in: *Omnia Terra*, 16 (1982), 248-254.

ROEST CROLLIUS A.A., *Inculturation and Incarnation. On speaking of the Christian faith and the cultures of humanity*, in: *Bulletin Secretariatus pro non-christianis*, 13 (1978), 134-140.

ROEST CROLLIUS A.A., *Inculturation and the meaning of culture*, in: *Gregorianum*, 61 (1980), 253-274.

ROEST CROLLIUS A.A., *What is so new about inculturation? A concept and its implications*, in: *Gregorianum*, 59 (1978), 721-738.

ROEST CROLLIUS A.A., *Per una teologia pratica dell'inculturazione*, in: *Inculturazione. Concetti, problemi, orientamenti*, Centrum Ignatianum Spiritualitatis, Roma, 1979, p. 36-53.

VANDANA, *Why so few contemplatives?*, in: *Vidyajyoti*, 42 (1978), 135-137.

ZAGO M., *Universal Church and Local Churches: Respective tasks in the encounter of the Gospel with cultures*, in: *FABC Papers*, n° 7, p. 8-17.

TIPOGRAFIA POLIGLOTTA DELLA PONTIFICIA UNIVERSITÀ GREGORIANA
PIAZZA DELLA PILOTTA, 4 - ROMA